THE LONDON MEDICINE

PHILIP DAVIES

First published in 2023 by:
Philip Davies
© Copyright 2023

The right of Philip Davies to be identified as the author of this work has been asserted by him in accordance with the Copyright, Designs and Patents Act 1988.

All Rights Reserved

No reproduction, copy or transmission of this publication may be made without written permission. No paragraph of this publication may be reproduced, copied or transmitted save with the written permission or in accordance with the provisions of the Copyright Act 1956 (as amended).

First Edition

ISBN: 978-1-915785-31-2

ebook: 978-1-915785-32-9

© Copyright 2023
Philip Davies

Printed and bound in Great Britain by:
Book Printing UK Remus House, Coltsfoot Drive, Woodston, Peterborough PE2 9BF

The London Medicine is the sequel to Funny Little Games, essential reading before reading this ongoing saga of celebrity musical composer Michael Maybrick. Born in Liverpool, Maybrick travelled Europe as an operatic baritone, before settling in London where he achieved celebrity status as a musical composer, achieving a high rank within Freemasonry, and mixing in influential social circles, including royalty.

But Michael Maybrick had a darker side, a narcissist with a dual personality and psychiatric disorder caused by an adolescent encounter with a Liverpool prostitute. Michael Maybrick was none other than the notorious Jack the Ripper, the serial killer responsible for murdering numerous prostitutes on the streets of Whitechapel. The victims met their deaths as the consequence of Maybrick's self-styled 'funny little games', in which they were carefully selected by their names, from which were plucked a gradually evolving anagram of Michael Maybrick's own name. A vengeful and macabre exorcism of his adolescent trauma, a deeply satisfying self revelation of his own name, in a code known only by the killer himself.

Now the mission was complete, the panic in Whitechapel had subsided, and all should have boded well for Michael Maybrick, destined for fame and fortune, with a knighthood in prospect, but a problem had arisen. Did his brother James nurture a suspicion of Michael's nefarious activities? Had James even mentioned his suspicions to his wife Florence, despised by Michael as an adulteress? There could only be one solution...

CHAPTERS

A Happy New Year	2
The London Medicine	18
Fly-Papers	28
Countdown	38
R.I.P	51
Baroness von Roques	60
The Brierley Letter	70
Inquest	77
Trial By Newspaper	90
Alice Mackenzie	101
The Blucher Letter	114
Snake In The Grass	122
A Regular Got-Up Case	135
The Missing Pill Box	146
Day Of Judgement	157
Mr R.F. Muckley	160
The Isle of Wight	169
Tom Merry	178
Mr. Miller	192
Old Friends	199
Cleveland Street	206
The Holy City	209
Till Death Do Us Part	218
Epilogue	228

THE VICTIMS

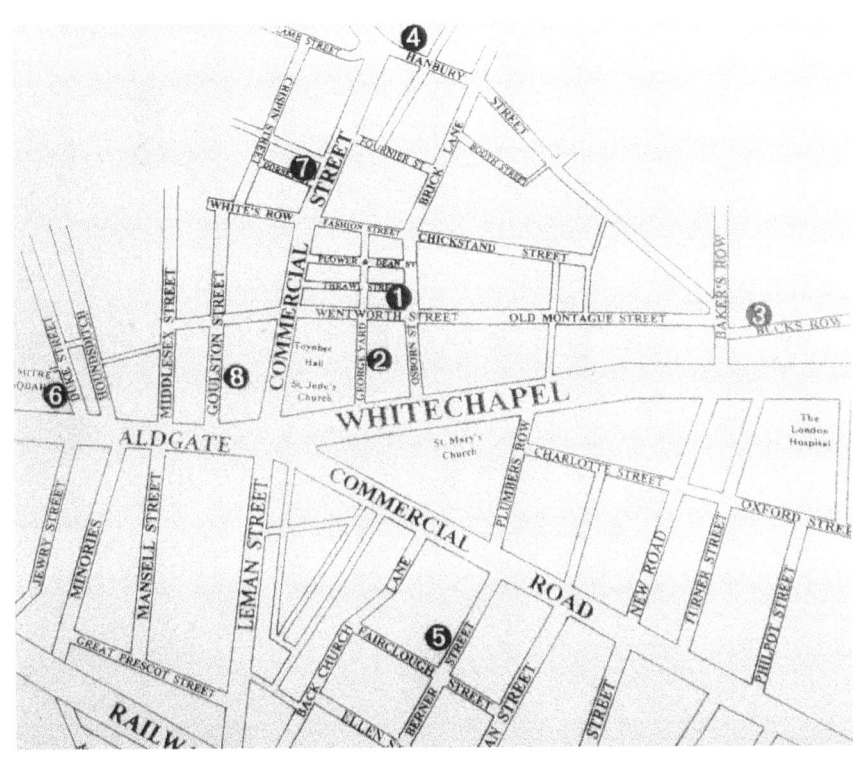

1. EMMA SMITH
2. MARTHA TABRAM
3. MARY ANN NICHOLS
4. ANNIE CHAPMAN
5. LIZ STRIDE
6. MARY ANN KELLY
(CATHERINE EDDOWES)
7. MARY JANE KELLY
8. ALICE MACKENZIE

THE LONDON MEDICINE

A HAPPY NEW YEAR

An uneasy calm descended over Whitechapel as the eventful year of 1888 drew to a close, and the name of Jack the Ripper began to evolve into legend. Two hundred miles away in Liverpool, Michael Maybrick was the house guest of brother James at Battlecrease House, where Florence, anticipating a frosty festive season, dutifully faded into the background, as expected of an obedient Victorian housewife.

James had been married for less than eight years, but, whilst in Michael's company, had a tendency to revert to bachelor status, a totally different person, resentful of marital ties to Florence, vulnerable to his brother's powers of coercion, and happy to boast of his extra-marital affairs. Just how far had Michael ventured in sharing his own fantasies over the years? Did James also entertain a masochistic streak, practiced on prostitutes prepared to indulge in sadistic fantasy at a price? Whilst working in Virginia, James was a regular visitor to a brothel owned by a Mary Hogwood, on record as stating,

I knew James Maybrick for several years, and up to the time of his marriage he called at my house, when in Norfolk, at least two or three times a week, and I saw him in his different moods and fancies. It was a common thing for him to take arsenic two or three times during the evening. He would pull from his pocket a small vial in which he carried his arsenic, and, putting a small quantity on his tongue, he would wash it down with a sip of wine. In fact, so often did he repeat this that I became afraid that if he died suddenly in my house, then some of us would be suspected of his murder. When drunk, Mr. James Maybrick would pour the powder into the palm of his hand, and lick it up with his tongue. I often cautioned him, but he answered 'Oh, I am used to it. It will not harm me.' Liverpool Citizen. 21 August 1889.

Another acquaintance of James's, whilst in Virginia, was master mariner Capt. John Fleming, who provides further commentary on James's propensity for arsenic.

I was in the said James Maybrick's office. He was cooking in a small pan over an oil stove, what I took to be hominy, a food much partaken in the southern states of America. I saw him deposit in the food a grey powder resembling light coloured pepper. He said to me, 'You would be horrified, I daresay, if you knew what this is.' I said, 'There's no harm in pepper,' and he answered 'It is arsenic.' I then said, 'Good God man, that is a deadly poison.' He, James Maybrick, said, 'We all take some poison, more or less, for instance I am now taking enough arsenic to kill you.' He then offered me a little of the compound, saying that a little would not hurt me, but I declined it, saying that I would not meddle in such a thing. He answered, 'I take this arsenic once in a while because it strengthens me.'

Just what were James's 'different moods and fancies' to which Mary Hogwood refers? Outrageous it may seem, but no-one seems to have considered the possibility that James, particularly when high on drugs, could have indulged in sexual fantasies. Just how did James pass his time when down in London? Did he physically assault Florence on occasions?

Was James, like Michael, subject to strange bouts of irrationality? There was a family precedent. Their uncle, another Michael Maybrick, brother to their father William, had spent the last months of his life as a patient in a mental institution in Old Swan, Liverpool. Very little attention appears to have been paid to James's idiosyncrasies, other than occasional references to 'extra-marital affairs' of which very little is known, but which could encompass a variety of activities. Michael would have taken great delight in fanning the embers, stoking the fires within, sharing alcoholic fantasies of how all women were whores, and should be treated as such. As always, Michael would have exploited the situation to his own advantage, seizing every opportunity to acquire material for a personal insurance policy, just in case. 'I actually find relief in writing. You should maintain a journal, and unburden your concerns.' James, ever mindful of pleasing his brother, mulled over the idea, and agreed to give the suggestion serious consideration. A diary might be a good idea, particularly if Michael approved.

By the time New Year's Eve arrived, Florence had come to realise just how much influence Michael exercised over her husband. On the 31st December, Florence penned a letter to her mother in Paris.

In his fury he tore up his will this morning, as he had me the sole legatee and trustee for the children in it. Now he proposes to settle everything he can on the children alone, allowing me only one third by law. I am sure it matters little to me, as long as the children are provided for. My own income will do for me alone. A pleasant way of commencing New Year.

Etched in Arsenic. Trevor Christie.

The friction within the marriage was now palpable, but little did Florence realise that the imminent New Year was about to become the worst year of her life. The days ticked by, with January and February as dull as any other year, with James pursuing his clandestine habit, and Florence, half his age, trapped with two adorable little children in a loveless marriage. Florence Aunspaugh, daughter of a close American friend of the Maybricks, remembered James well.

You would not term him a handsome man. He had a fine forehead, very pleasant intellectual face and an open, honest countenance, light, sandy coloured hair, grey eyes, and a florid complexion. He had none of that blunt, abrupt manner so characteristic of the English, but was exceedingly cultured, polished and refined in his manners, and was a superb host. But there were two unfortunate features in his make-up. That was his morose, gloomy disposition, and extremely high temper. He also imagined he was afflicted with every ailment to which the flesh is heir. Yes, Mr. Maybrick was an arsenic addict. He craved it like a narcotic fiend. He used it right in our home. He was always after the doctor to prescribe it, and the druggist to make him up a tonic with arsenic in it. He once said to my mother, 'They only give me enough to aggravate and worry me, and make me always craving for more.' He was always taking strychnine tablets, and was great on beef broth and arsenic. My father once said, 'Maybrick has got a dozen drug stores in his stomach.'

Letters of Florence Aunspaugh to Trevor Christie.
University of Wyoming, Laramie.

'A narcotic fiend with a high temper, yet polished and refined in manners,' does tend to portray James, just like Michael, as being capable of harbouring multiple personalities, with the effects of his addiction causing Florence, three months earlier, in November 1888, to confide in the family doctor, Arthur Hopper, about James's 'habit of taking a strong medicine, which had a bad influence on him.' At around the same time, James consulted a separate medical practitioner, Dr. J. Drysdale, on five separate occasions, complaining of headaches and numbness down the left leg and hand. According to the doctor, on being asked what medicines he had been in the habit of taking, James listed nitro-hydrochloric acid, strychnine, hydrate of potash and several other drugs, but on no occasion was he prepared to admit to taking arsenic.

Then, in late February 1889, James met salesman Valentine Blake, in Liverpool promoting the sale of ramie fibre, a potential substitute for cotton in the manufacture of fabrics, and, in the course of conversation, it was revealed that the manufacturing process involved the use of arsenic. When Blake let slip that he had in his possession a quantity of arsenic, James immediately offered to promote ramie fibre on the Cotton Exchange, on the basis that Blake's available supply of arsenic would surreptitiously end up in James's possession. The deal was struck, and around 150 grains of arsenic changed hands. In Blake's own words,

I told him to be careful, as he had almost enough to poison a regiment. When we separated, James Maybrick took away the arsenic with him, saying he was going home to his house in Aigburth.
Affidavit. Valentine Blake.

This was probably the first drug deal on Merseyside, only coming to light twelve months later. 150 grains constitute a serious amount of arsenic, and Valentine Blake's inference was that James must have secreted the stache at Battlecrease House, where Florence Aunspaugh provides a unique insight into the Maybricks' lifestyle,

Battlecrease was a palatial home. The grounds must have consisted of five or six acres, and were given most excellent care. There were large trees, luxuriant shrubbery, and flowerbeds. Dotted around the grounds were little rock nooks or summer houses with seats, covered with old English ivy and other running vines. A conservatory was near the house, and a pair of peacocks roamed the grounds. Running through the grounds was a small natural stream of water, part of which had been broadened and deepened to form a lake. This pond was stocked with fish, and swans and ducks were swimming on the surface. Mr. Maybrick was very fond of hunting, and had quite a few dogs. I saw six horses, a pair of handsome looking blacks which were always hitched to the carriage, a pair of greys, which were hitched to what they called a trap, and two saddle horses, one Mr. Maybrick used and the other Mrs. Maybrick.

Letters of Florence Aunspaugh to Trevor Christie.
University of Wyoming, Laramie.

By now, the Maybricks' delicate marital situation was compounded by financial problems, resulting mainly from James's insistence on keeping up appearances. Theirs was a costly lifestyle, with expensive overheads resulting in a financial overload, of which a contributing factor was Florence's predilection for retail therapy to the point of extravagance, all based on credit, and for the main part unbeknown to James. Soon, demand notes began to arrive at the house, intercepted by Florence, who was reduced to pawning jewellery, and borrowing from moneylenders to settle the accounts. In a letter to her mother in Paris, Florence wrote,

I am utterly worn out, and in such a state of overstrained nervousness I am hardly fit for anything. Whenever the doorbell rings, I feel ready to faint for fear it is someone coming to have an account paid, and when James comes home at night, it is with fear and trembling that I look into his face to see whether anyone has been to the office about my bills ... my life is a continual state of fear of something or somebody. There is no way of stemming the current. I would gladly give up the house tomorrow, and move somewhere else, but Jim says it would ruin him outright, for one must keep up appearances until he has more capital to fall back on to meet his liabilities, since the least suspicion aroused, all claims would pour in at once, and how could Jim settle with what he has now?

Florence Maybrick.

This was not the idyllic, sophisticated lifestyle envisaged by Florence on the S.S. Baltic in mid-Atlantic, or on her wedding day in Piccadilly, made worse by a lack of real friends in Liverpool. Well aware of James's occasional intakes of white powder, on or around the 12th March, Florence wrote a letter to Michael, the precise contents of which are unknown, as Michael claimed to have destroyed the letter. Perhaps the letter contained a plea for financial assistance? What is known for certain, by Michael's own admission, is that Florence wrote of James's illicit intake of powders, which in her mind may have been the cause of his persistent headaches. Michael's officially recorded response was that when he raised the matter with James on the occasion of a weekend visit to London one week later, James's response was 'Whoever told you that? It is a damned lie.' It is, however, inconceivable that the topic was not pursued, as the brothers had two full days in London in which to discuss Florence's allegation. James had confided in friends of his arsenic addiction, yet Michael, accomplished and convincing liar, would repeatedly claim that their conversation on the subject ended there and then. So far as Michael was concerned, the content of their fraternal discussions was nobody else's business, and if James denied taking arsenic, so be it.

As well as expressing concern over James's ongoing drug problem, Florence had also learned of his extra marital activities, although uncertain with whom, by which time she too was not averse to flirtation, and, whilst maintaining a secret bond with Edwin, soon developed an illicit association with Alfred Brierley, a cotton broker twelve years younger than James, trading at the same Liverpool Cotton Exchange. The mutual attraction had not passed unnoticed in the workplace, however, and word eventually filtered through to Edwin, who had little option but to sulk in silence. Likewise, Matilda Brigg's spinster sister, Gertrude Janion, who had also been casting eyes at Alfred, was not amused. The gloom of winter gradually dissipated with the welcome onset of spring, and one day, on returning home early, Florence found the children playing unattended in the garden, with children's nurse Alice Yapp pre-occupied in gossiping with the kitchen staff. A confrontation ensued, in which Alice was given a humiliating dressing down in front of the other servants, resulting in an unforgiving resentment within the young servant girl, whose upbringing did not readily relate to subservience, despite her position within the household. After all, Alice had been interviewed personally by Mr. Maybrick, not his wife, who was only the same age as she was. Alice was deeply offended, and would not forget.

Michael in the meantime, content with the outcome of his funny little games in Whitechapel, toured the country as Mr. Maybrick and Stephen Adams, counting down the hours to his big day at United Grand Lodge in April, yet still mulling over how to deal with Florence Maybrick. He had thoroughly enjoyed desecrating Florence's lookalike in Miller's Court, but in reality she was still very much alive, with those penetrating blue eyes, empty and expressionless perhaps, but potentially dangerous, as only Michael Maybrick understood. One light-hearted and innocuous remark made by Florence over dinner at Christmas, after two glasses of claret, had hinted that Michael could be the Whitechapel Murderer. Intended as frivolity and accepted as such by all present, the remark had nonetheless struck home. This woman could bring about his downfall, should she just once voice her light-hearted banter in Liverpool social circles. Florence definitely had to go. It was pre-destined anyway, and now it was just a matter of how and when this could be achieved, without incriminating himself.

In March 1889, Florence duly obliged by elevating her flirtations with Alfred Brierley into an adulterous relationship, with apparent disregard for the consequences. Florence covertly telegrammed a reservation at Flatman's Hotel, Covent Garden, under the name of Mr. and Mrs. Thomas Maybrick, Manchester, for the weekend of the 23th March, at the same time arranging to liaise, whilst in London, with family friend John Baillie Knight, to discuss arrangements for a potential separation from James. The love tryst was a momentous move, spontaneously undertaken with unaccountable lack of forethought, and even less intelligence. Alfred Brierley may well have been unmarried, eligible, and captivated by Florence's seductive looks, but Florence was married, and Brierley worked alongside her husband in the Liverpool Cotton Exchange, where rumours were already beginning to circulate.

Brierley turned up at Flatman's Hotel the day after Florence, whereupon, for whatever reason, the intended love affair metamorphosed into disaster, with Brierley losing his nerve after half-heartedly spending the night together, and catching the train back to Liverpool the following day. Florence, recklessly infatuated, was understandably distraught, and John Baillie Knight arranged for her to stay with his aunt Margaret over the next few days, during which time he arranged for Florence to contact a firm of solicitors, who drafted a letter of proposed separation, on the grounds of James's adultery. The letter was never delivered.

Sunday the 25th March 1889, was to provide Michael Maybrick with yet another platform for furthering his prospects of social advancement, on the occasion of the opening of the new headquarters of the 20th Middlesex (Artists) Rifle Volunteers. Lieutenant Maybrick was responsible for directing the entertainment in the presence of HRH Edward, Prince of Wales, Grand Master of English Freemasonry, four weeks before Brother Maybrick would be presented to the Prince for investiture as Grand Organist of the United Grand Lodge of England.

On that same evening, with Brierley safely back home in Liverpool, Florence was wined and dined at the Grand Hotel and Gaiety Theatre by John Baillie Knight, and on the next, incredibly, by Michael Maybrick, offering an evening of in-depth conversation at the Café Royal, with a very understanding and concerned psychopathic serial killer, intent on her demise.

The day after she was with Brierley in London, I took her to dine out at the Café Royal in Regent's Park, and took her to the theatre. She has come to me time and again for money, and always got it.

Michael Maybrick.

Florence had visited Michael at his home address at Wellington Mansions, Regent's Park, just down the road from the Café Royal, a meeting of desperation, with little thought for the consequences. If the statement is true, and monetary dialogue had taken place between the pair on more than one occasion, the social butterfly had fluttered into a very tangled web indeed. An expert at psychological manipulation, Michael would have drawn on the occasion by helping Florence unburden her problems, gleaning whatever information was on offer, and soon confirming that which he had already suspected, that not only was Florence foolish and impulsive, as proven by the weekend's events at Flatman's Hotel, but she and James had indeed harboured light-hearted but foolish fantasies that Michael Maybrick may have been Jack the Ripper. After an evening at the Café Royal, however, Florence would have been totally reassured by the mass murderer's convincing pretence of sincerity and empathy, soon realising how silly she had been for nurturing such suspicions. Michael could be a really understanding person, and Florence told him so.

On Florence's return to Liverpool on the 28th March, nothing untoward appears to have happened, and, before very long, fear and apprehension were replaced by complacency. On the following day, James and Florence attended the Grand National at Aintree, where, in an outstanding display of ineptitude, Florence drifted away from James, and consorted arm in arm with Alfred Brierley. Once home at Battlecrease House, she was confronted by her furious husband, fearful of scandal, overwhelmed with rage, and engulfed by a full day's intake of alcohol and noxious substances. His brother's cultivated vilification of Florence, simmering inside James's head, was fully released, and a serious confrontation ensued, with Florence threatening to walk out, following which James was heard to shout 'Florie, I never thought it would come to this. By heavens, if you cross that threshold, you shall never enter this house again.'

That night, James Maybrick, the 'narcotic fiend with a high temper', displayed his true colours, and Florence awoke the following morning with a black eye. The first person she turned to was Matilda Briggs, at whose suggestion the pair went to see Dr. Hopper, to whom Florence recounted the incident in graphic detail, confiding that James was having a secret affair, and confessing to serious financial indebtedness, which would inevitably lead to further disruption of the marriage, if and when discovered. As a longstanding personal friend of James, Dr. Hopper somehow managed to broker a reconciliation, with James promising to honour Florence's debts. Another tiff occurred the following day, however, after which Florence complained of feeling unwell, resulting in the cook running off to summon the local general practitioner, Dr. Richard Humphreys. All was not well at Battlecrease House, and the clock was ticking with a grim inevitability, as James's drug habit developed into a serious addiction, resulting in repeated bouts of illness and irritability, which he refused to acknowledge were the consequence of his poisonous intake.

A grain of arsenic is the size of a peppercorn, and two are sufficient to kill a man. When incorporated into legally available medicines, arsenic content was measured in drops, with a hundred drops per grain, the average prescription dose containing four drops. Local chemist Edwin Heaton, operating close to the Liverpool Cotton Exchange, was the source of James Maybrick's legitimate but limited supply of 'recreational' arsenic, in the form of liquor arsenicalis, later confirming that over a ten year period, James's daily prescription dose had increased from four to seven drops, and, when James went away on business trips, he would make up packages varying from eight to sixteen doses.

He used to call continually at my shop, sometimes four or five times a day, for what he called his 'pick-me-up', but which was liquid arsenicalis.
Edward Heaton.

Two weeks after the Grand National, James travelled to London to stay with Michael over two successive weekends on the 14th and 21st April, possibly with a view to arranging settlement of Florence's debts, which by now had been discreetly transferred to two London moneylenders. Evenings spent together over brandies in Michael's sumptuous drawing room would invariably have centred around Florence, guided by the host into alcohol fuelled fantasies of the ideal solution, which, of course, would never be fulfilled. James was well used to Michael's mood swings, which indeed had given rise to his own suspicions of Michael's Whitechapel involvement, a source of much amusement whenever the topic had been raised. James simply did not realise how distinctly unamused Michael actually was, as he laughed off the suggestion. Michael was his mentor, was always right, always had been, and how thoroughly enjoyable it was just to fantasise between themselves over what Florence really deserved. An invariable topic of discussion during more rational moments would have been James's obsessional fear of infirmity, as a consequence of which Michael obligingly introduced him to his own physician, Dr. Charles Fuller, who diagnosed severe indigestion, much to James's disappointment as a confirmed hypochondriac, writing out two prescriptions which James took back to Liverpool, for preparation by his local chemists.

James Maybrick had been initiated into Freemasonry in 1870 into St. George's Lodge of Harmony No.32, meeting at the Adelphi Hotel, in Liverpool, subsequently joining the Lodge's associated Jerusalem Chapter No.32 two years later. Whilst in London, Michael would undoubtedly have taken the opportunity of inviting James to the Masonic Hall in Great Queen Street, where rehearsals would have been under way for the forthcoming Grand Investiture, introducing him to his contemporary Grand Officers, including the Lord Chamberlain, the Earl of Lathom, Deputy Grand Master of the United Grand Lodge of England, Provincial Grand Master of Lancashire, and senior member of James Maybrick's own Lodge. Perhaps whilst James was engaged in conversation elsewhere, Michael chose a discreet moment to quietly confide in the Lord Chamberlain his concern that brother James had been behaving somewhat strangely over the last few months on the occasion of his trips to London, and just perhaps he might have been connected to the murders in Whitechapel. Just perhaps, but worthy of mention?

The Earl of Lathom would undoubtedly have been totally nonplussed at such a remark, preposterous, yet presented with such embarrassed humility by a truly just and upright man, that it could only have been made as the result of much soul searching. Speculation was rife throughout the nation as to the possible identity of the Whitechapel Murderer, and innocent men were being unjustly named as suspects on a regular basis, yet why else would this highly trustworthy man jeopardise his reputation by making such an allegation against his own brother, without possessing a genuine belief in its authenticity?

Three days later on Wednesday 24th April 1889, the Annual Investiture Ceremony of the United Grand Lodge of England took place before a select audience of 1700 Freemasons in full masonic regalia, followed by a resplendent procession into the adjoining banqueting hall, to the resounding tones of the mighty Grand Lodge organ. Poignantly, seated at the dining table close to the newly appointed Grand Organist was the recently knighted Bro. Sir Polydore de Keyser, the first Roman Catholic Lord Mayor of London, whose outgoing celebrations in November had been marred by the horrific murder of Mary Jane Kelly. Also nearby was Bro. Henry Homewood Crawford, newly appointed Grand Steward and City of London Solicitor, acting on behalf of the police at the inquest of Catherine Eddowes, alias Mary Ann Kelly.

The appointments at Grand Lodge were as follows,

Grand Master	Bro. HRH The Prince of Wales
Deputy Grand Master	Bro. The Earl of Lathom
Secretary	Bro. Thomas Shadwell Clarke
Grand Senior Warden	Bro. Lord George Hamilton
Grand Junior Warden	Bro. Sir John Eldon Gorst M.P.
Grand Chaplain	Bro. Rev. Francis Byng
Grand Treasurer	Bro. Edward Terry
Grand Registrar Q.C.	Bro. Judge Adolphus Philbrick
Grand Senior Deacons	Bro. Sir Lionel Davell
	Bro. Sir Polydore de Keyser
Grand Junior Deacons	Bro. Col. Addison Potter C.B.
	Bro. Charles Chester Cheston
Grand Superintendent of Works	Bro. Col. R.W. Edis
Grand Director of Ceremonies	Bro. Sir Albert Woods (Garter)
Grand Sword Bearer	Bro. Eugene Montenuis
Grand Organist	Bro. Michael Maybrick
Grand Assistant Secretary	Bro. A. A. Pendlebury
Grand Tyler	Bro. D. Sadler

Grand Steward	Bro. H. Homewood Crawford

Michael Maybrick was in his element, divinely protected, truly unassailable on a mission guided by angelic providence, with not one soul present having the slightest idea the most wanted man in the land was in their midst. From his position to the right of the Grand Master, the Earl of Lathom quietly watched, still undecided what to make of Bro. Maybrick, strangely detached, yet with the uncanny ability to instantly charm, even the normally aloof Sir Polydore de Keyser. Could his brother James really be Jack the Ripper? Best let the matter rest for the time being.

THE LONDON MEDICINE

On James's return to Liverpool on Monday the 22nd April, family life at Battlecrease House continued as usual, with both parties publicly maintaining the pretence of a happy marriage. In a few days time, Florence and James were due to attend a Masquerade Ball, the kind of social pageant in which Florence had delighted whilst in Alabama, and personal appearance was, as always, of paramount importance. Habitual visits to the up-market milliners and haberdashers of Liverpool's Bold Street, no expense spared, had ensured that Florence would be the belle of the ball, but an embarrassing problem had surfaced, quite literally. Acne had begun to appear on Florence's otherwise flawless face, and remedial measures were necessary. Back home in Alabama, the family physician, Dr. Greggs, would have prescribed the usual face wash of elderflower water, tincture of benzoin and a drop or two of arsenic, which would usually alleviate the outbreak within two or three days. Similarly, when the young Florence had been in Germany, her friends would have made their own cosmetic solution of lavender water, elderflower water, and fly-papers, containing small amounts of arsenic, to make a similar preparation. So Florence accordingly went about buying fly-papers from a local chemist in Liverpool, and preparing a lotion to assuage the unsightly spots.

On Friday the 26th April, four days after James's return from London, there arrived in the post at Battlecrease House a parcel, postmarked London, containing a bottle of medicine, labelled Nux Vomica. Dr. Fuller was later to state categorically that he had only provided James Maybrick with two written prescriptions which, on his return to Liverpool, were presented to local chemists Clay and Abraham. The parcel definitely did not emanate from Dr. Fuller, so who sent the mysterious bottle, why, and what did it contain? Housemaid Mary Cadwallader was adamant that the London Medicine did not arrive unexpectedly.

Mr. Maybrick told me that he had been up to London, and was expecting medicine a day or two before it arrived.
Mary Cadwallader.

On the afternoon following receipt of the medicine, James was due to attend a race meeting on the Wirral, on the opposite side of the River Mersey, but in the morning became ill, and in the words of the children's nurse, Alice Yapp,

I remember Mr. Maybrick going to the Wirral Races on the 27th April, and after he had gone, between ten o' clock and eleven o' clock, Mrs. Maybrick came to me and said, 'Master has been taking an overdose of medicine. It is strychnine, and very dangerous. He is very ill.' I said, 'What medicine is it?' and she said, 'Some which has been presented by a doctor in London.'
Alice Yapp.

James and Florence clearly believed that the medicine had been sent by Dr. Fuller, but the doctor would later confirm that he had provided written prescriptions only, and those for harmless indigestion remedies. On arrival at work that Saturday morning, James had confided to office clerk, George Smith, that he was feeling unwell,

He said that he had taken an overdose of medicine, and there was strychnine in it, that he was on the W.C. for an hour, and all his limbs were stiff and he could not move.
George Smith.

James was an authority on the taste and effects of strychnine, and was unequivocally of the opinion that such was the content of the mysterious London Medicine. Just as Michael had anticipated, James could not resist that extra dose, resulting in the symptoms described by George Smith. During his visit to London, James had also come into possession of certain pills which were definitely unrelated to Dr. Fuller's prescriptions, and which he had reason to believe had originally been prescribed for Michael. Dr. Fuller would later confirm that James ....

.... had been taking a pill which he said I had prescribed for his brother. This, however, is not the case. I had not prescribed it. He told me of nothing else he had been taking. I asked him if he had been taking any medicine, and he said the pill was the only thing he had been taking.

Dr. Charles Fuller.

Just what was the mysterious pill of which the doctor had no knowledge, but which James attributed to his brother? The answer may well be provided by an article in the Liverpool Weekly Post a month later.

It was freely rumoured that Mr. Maybrick had told a friend of his, living in the neighbourhood, that he had taken an overdose of medicine which contained poison, and that he felt the worse for it. We are able to give the true story which gave rise to this rumour on the authority of the gentleman himself, who got it at first hand. It appears that it had been apparent to his friends on the Exchange that for many weeks past Mr. Maybrick had been seriously ill. He had been petulant in his manner and very delicate in appearance, as compared with his usual state of health. Some weeks ago he went up to London to consult a leading physician as to his ailment, and this gentleman, in addition to some other medicine, prescribed for him certain pills. Mr. Maybrick took them, and told a friend that he did not rely on the specified dose, namely two pills, but had taken four, and had felt much worse for it. He made a second visit to London, and upon this occasion the physician told him that he had done great wrong in doubling the dose, because the pills consisted largely of strychnine.

Liverpool Weekly Post. 25 May 1889.

The story certainly conforms to the known facts, even down to James's deterioration in health since his secret dockside arsenic deal with Valentine Blake. James incorrectly believed the strychnine based pills had been prescribed for Michael by Dr. Fuller, but it appears Michael had given James the pills without Dr. Fuller's involvement, confirmed on James's next visit to the doctor, one week later, when he explained to James the strychnine content of the pills he had been taking. The doctor must have been mystified by this strange sequence of events, and without doubt would have raised the subject with Michael, but no further reference is made to this matter. James, of course, was quite content with this useful supplement to his usual drug habit, suspecting no ulterior motive, and subsequently confiding his intake of the pills to a close friend and work colleague on the Exchange, very likely his lifelong pal George Davidson, who would prove not only concerned with James's welfare, but sufficiently suspicious of this strange sequence of events as to contact the press, hence the newspaper article. James was under the total misapprehension that both the pills and the London Medicine were legitimate prescriptions emanating from Dr. Fuller, rather than substances insidiously introduced by his own brother.

The London Medicine arrived on the morning of the day of the Wirral Races, which, despite severe weather conditions,

James was determined to attend. The outing involved a long journey on horseback, including arduous ferry crossings over the River Mersey, and this foolhardy venture was about to take its toll, with later witness statements confirming James's odd behaviour during the day, and noting his fragility. Racetrack acquaintance William Thomson commented on James's unsteadiness in the saddle, only to receive the response that it was due to his having taken a 'double dose' that morning. Likewise, fellow spectator and friend Morden Rigg expressed no surprise to hear of James's intake of strychnine that morning, as he was always taking medicines of one kind or another.

He turned round to my wife's carriage, and told her he had taken an overdose of strychnine that morning, and that his limbs were quite rigid. She is prepared to testify this, if necessary.

Morden Rigg.

James remained on the Wirral that evening, dining at the residence of his friends the Hobsons, where his lack of co-ordination at the table was noted by the hosts.

After coming from the races, he went to dine with a friend, and whilst there his hands were so unsteady and twitching, that he upset some wine, and he was greatly distressed lest his friends would think he was drunk.

Dr. Richard Humphreys.

On arriving home at Battlecrease House later that night, after a gruelling return journey on horseback in heavy rain, James collapsed into bed, and on awaking the following morning, complained of severe chest pains and partial paralysis. Dr. Humphreys was summoned, diagnosing severe indigestion as the result of a heavy day at the races. In the course of conversation, Florence made a point of telling the doctor about the white powder which she had seen James taking on previous occasions, but, when subsequently approached on the subject, James's response was outright denial, which Dr. Humphreys chose to accept. James remained poorly, and was confined to bed throughout Sunday 28th, being visited in the afternoon by Edwin, newly arrived from America, and residing in rented rooms in Rodney Street, near the city centre.

With only two days to go to the Masquerade Ball on Tuesday, it was decided that Edwin should take the place of James, to which Florence acceded with concealed delight. Accustomed as she was to the lively social scene in Alabama, and whilst still looking forward to Edwin's company at the Ball, Florence was, however, rather apprehensive as to the suitability of such an event in Liverpool, confiding to her mother in Paris,

We are asked to a Ball Masque, which, being given in Liverpool, and the people provincials, I hardly think likely to be a success. A certain amount of 'diablerie', wit and life is always required at an entertainment of this sort, and as it will be quite a novel innovation, people will hardly know what is expected of them.

Florence had every intention of being noticed at the event, and on Monday 29th April paid another visit to a local chemist, purchasing more fly-papers and a lotion containing elderflower and benzoin, which she mixed in a basin in her bedroom. On that same day, James wrote a letter to brother Michael, addressing him as 'Blucher', yet another pseudonym, earned by his resemblance to Prince Gebhard von Blucher, the ice cold, arrogant and militarily precise

Prussian general, who had distinguished himself at the Battle of Waterloo.

My Dear Blucher, Liverpool, 29th April.

I have been very seedy indeed. On Saturday morning I found my legs getting stiff and useless but by sheer strength of will shook off the feeling and went down on horseback to Wirral Races, and dined with the Hobsons. Yesterday morning I felt more like dying than living, so much that Florie called in another doctor who said it was an acute attack of indigestion and gave me something to relieve the alarming symptoms, so all went well until about 8 o'clock. I went to bed and had lain there one hour by myself and was reading on my back. Many times I felt a twitching but took little notice of it thinking it would pass away but instead of doing so I got worse and worse and in trying to move around to ring the bell I found I could not do so, but finally managed it but by the time Florie and Edwin could get upstairs I was stiff, and for two mortal hours my legs were like bars of iron stretched out to the fullest extent but rigid as steel. The doctor came finally again, but could not make it indigestion this time, and the conclusion he came to was that the Nux Vomica I had been taking under Dr. Fuller had poisoned me as all the symptoms warranted such a conclusion. I know I am today sore from head to feet and played out completely. What is the matter with me? None of the doctors so far can make out, and I suppose never will until I am stretched out and cold, then future generations may profit by it if they hold a post mortem which I am quite willing they should do.

I don't think I will come up to London this week, as I don't feel much like travelling and cannot go on with Fuller's physic yet a while, but I will come up again and see him shortly. Edwin does not join you just yet but he will write you himself. I suppose you go to your country quarters on Wednesday? With love,

Your affectionate brother,

Jim.

So what can be deduced from this letter other than the fact that James was in complete denial of his symptoms being due to his intake of illicit substances? It has already been established that Dr. Fuller wrote out two prescriptions for James, which were later prepared for him in Liverpool, and collected in person on the 24th April. Mr. Christopher Robinson, the chemist who made up the prescriptions confirmed that neither contained arsenic. James had evidently deduced, however, that the 'London Medicine', which he believed emanated from Dr. Fuller, was the source of his latest bout of ill health. The 'London Medicine', referred to as Nux Vomica in James's letter, had arrived by post on the 26th April, and the next day, following James's intake of that medicine, his condition had deteriorated rapidly as described in his letter, to the extent that Dr. Humphreys concluded that the medication sent by Dr. Fuller had been poisoning him. That is a very serious allegation indeed. It is worth examining the content of this strychnine based Victorian concoction.

The effects of Nux Vomica in small doses are those of a bitter tonic, with an influence on the nervous functions which is quite peculiar, and which, in its higher degrees, is so violent and dangerous as to give the medicine a place among the poisons. From very small doses, no effects are at first experienced, but if repeated, they will increase the appetite, hasten digestion and generally act the part of a simple tonic. When it is taken more largely than requisite for the tonic effect, an entirely new series of phenomena are developed. The first observable effect is a feeling of stiffness in the muscles of the jaw, or of weakness with trembling of the limbs. After a time, the feeling of stiffness may be experienced elsewhere, upon any attempt at movement. Along with this symptom, there is an increased sensitiveness, so that a light tap upon the skin will produce sudden and involuntary startings of the muscles, and twitchings in the limbs. Under a more energetic influence of the medicine, the muscular stiffness increases and extends, so that the patient complains not only of rigidity of the limbs, but of tightness about the throat.

A Treatise on Therapeutics and Pharmacology. George B. Wood.

Just like Dr. Humphreys, James was clearly under the misconception that Dr. Fuller was inadvertently poisoning him with the high strychnine content of the Nux Vomica. Someone certainly had that intention. Never having been content with a standard dose, James would have gulped down the fluid just as expected, but was also double dosing. James had confided to friends of having taken illicit substances over the years, including strychnine, and it is fair to assume that from time to time he would have over-dosed to limited degrees whilst seeking the optimum high, and would have been familiar with the after affects. In this latest instance, however, James had told his clerk, George Smith, that he had taken strychnine, and was experiencing stiff limbs and a temporary inability to moved. Why then was James, in his letter to Michael, so mystified by the latest symptoms? James quite simply had never taken such a concentrated overdose of strychnine before in his life, on top of the pills Michael had so generously given him a few days earlier. The average man, unaccustomed to substance abuse, would have been laid out dead. Such indeed was the plan, but James's constitution was programmed for resistance, and by the 1st May he was back at work, weak, but determined to carry on life as normal.

Meanwhile, two hundred miles away, Michael Maybrick, pacing the floor of his residence in Regent's Park, could only speculate on the outcome of the medical treat he had posted to his brother.

FLY-PAPERS

On Wednesday, the 1st May, James had recovered sufficiently to resume work at the Cotton Exchange, but still felt decidedly jaded. That evening, the Maybricks entertained brother Edwin and an old acquaintance of ten years standing, Captain Peter John Irving of the White Star Line, who was due to set sail in the course of the next few days. Captain Irving would later recall querying James's strange behaviour, to which Edwin responded, 'Oh, he's killing himself with that damned strychnine.' An off the cuff remark, but an open admission by Edwin that he was well aware of James's intake of the drug, an admission which would later be denied.

James attended the Cotton Exchange on Thursday and Friday, but his condition was beginning to deteriorate, and by Saturday he was confined to bed, where his condition fluctuated daily. On the morning of Tuesday the 7th, Dr. Humphreys found James in fine fettle, exclaiming 'Humphreys, I am quite a different man altogether today', as a consequence of which Dr. Humphreys left Battlecrease House feeling quite content that his treatment was proving successful. Florence, however, was still concerned at James's condition, and telegraphed Edwin at the Cotton Exchange, requesting another doctor be summoned for a second opinion. Edwin duly called on Dr. William Carter, a respected Liverpool physician based close to his own lodgings in Rodney Street, who diagnosed James as suffering from diarrhoea and vomiting, 'as might be produced by an irritant poison', a medical expression covering a variety of items including bad food and wine, and not necessarily poison in the conventional meaning of the word. Edwin also sent a telegram to Michael, advising that James was seriously ill, just the news Michael was waiting for.

On the following morning, Wednesday the 8th May, James's condition was once again a cause for concern, and Florence sent for Dr. Humphreys, following which it was agreed that Florence should send a telegram to the Nurses Institution, requesting the services of a professional nurse, in response to which Nurse Ellen Gore arrived at 3.00 p.m. Matilda Briggs was next to arrive, accompanied by her sister Martha Hughes, being met in the garden by the children's nurse, Alice Yapp, who, in Mrs. Briggs's words, 'made a statement to her.' On entering the house and encountering Florence, Mrs. Briggs explained that she had received a telegram the previous evening from Michael in London, advising that Edwin had notified him James was ill, and requesting her to call at the house. Mrs. Briggs then sent a telegram of her own to Michael, saying, 'Come at once. Strange things going on here.' An interesting insight into the two main female players in this unfolding scenario is provided by the ever perceptive Florence Aunspaugh,

Both Mrs Briggs and Nurse Yapp despised and hated Mrs. Maybrick, and the most pathetic part about it was that Mrs. Maybrick did not have the brain to realise their attitude towards her. Mrs. Briggs was a woman near Mr. Maybrick's age, and my father was told that she had been madly in love with him, and had made a desperate effort to marry him. Mrs. Briggs took all kinds of authority around the place, and with the servants. She would address Mr. Maybrick as James. Not one time did she ever address Mrs. Maybrick. Nurse Yapp was a very efficient, capable woman, but also a most deceitful and treacherous one.

Letters of Florence Aunspaugh to Trevor Christie.
University of Wyoming, Laramie.

Few people had a good word for Alice Yapp, including the Maybricks' former children's nurse, Emma Parkes.

Our representative interviewed on Saturday evening the nurse who was with Mrs. Maybrick when both her children were born, and who left to get married at the time Alice Yapp came. She spoke of the affectionate terms upon which Mr. and Mrs. Maybrick were during the five years she was with them. The former nurse speaks of Yapp as having been of an extremely prying nature, and says that on several occasions she opened letters, and that as soon as Mrs. Maybrick's back was turned she went prying about in her room. Perhaps Yapp considered it a servant's privilege to open her mistress's communications.
Liverpool Courier. 17 August 1889.

James Maybrick had travelled all the way to Southport to personally secure the services of Alice Yapp, the same age as his wife, and unattached. Alice was a deeply embittered young lady, resentful of Florence's status, possibly enamoured of James, and still fuming at her humiliation by Florence some weeks earlier, in front of the other servants. Alice was also adept at telling lies. What precisely was her 'statement' to Mrs. Briggs that morning, which sent her scurrying off to telegraph Michael with the instruction, no less, that he should come from London to Liverpool, post haste? The housemaid, Bessie Brierley, had noticed fly-papers soaking in Florence's bedroom wash-basin, as a facial preparation prior to the Masked Ball, and had mentioned this to the other servants. The fantasist Alice Yapp had then embellished the discovery, and drawn her own dramatic and vindictive conclusion that Florence was poisoning James with arsenic distilled from the fly-papers, as a consequence of which Florence's life was about to be changed forever.

In a later interview with the Liverpool Daily Post, Mrs. Briggs relayed her version of the conversation with Alice that morning.

On Tuesday, May 7th, I received a telegram from Mr. Michael Maybrick, informing me that his brother was ill, and requesting me to go and see him. On the following morning my sister, Mrs. Hughes, and myself went to his residence. Nurse Yapp beckoned us across the lawn, and said to me, 'Thank God, Mrs. Briggs, you have come, for the mistress is poisoning the master. For goodness sake, go and see him for yourselves.' Mrs. Hughes asked her what reason she had for saying this, as it was an awful accusation to make, and she then told us about the fly-papers, and how food intended for Mr. Maybrick had been tampered with by his wife. We were so shocked by what she said that we went up at once to his bedroom. Mrs. Maybrick followed us immediately, and was apparently angry, telling us we had no right there, but if we would go downstairs she would let us know all about his symptoms.

Liverpool Daily Post. 14 August 1889.

Only five years earlier, Liverpool had been shaken by what came to be known as the 'Flannagan Case', in which two sisters, Margaret Higgins and Catherine Flannagan, had been found guilty of poisoning Mrs. Higgins's husband by arsenic, brewed from fly-papers. Both were hanged at Walton Gaol.

One week after the interview with Mrs. Briggs, the same reporter managed to obtain an interview with Alice Yapp, included in which was an outright denial of Mrs. Brigg's version of events, despite the conversation having been witnessed by Mrs. Hughes.

I never said to Mrs. Briggs, as she has stated, that the mistress was poisoning the master.

Liverpool Daily Post. 20 August 1889.

Someone was lying. Alexander MacDougall later interviewed the two servants who were in the kitchen that morning, when Alice Yapp was present.

I have questioned Mary Cadwallader and Elizabeth Humphreys about these 'suspicious circumstances.' They say that Alice Yapp might have been in the kitchen when they were talking about sugar in the bread and milk, but they are confident they said nothing to her about any soup, or bread, or things tasting differently. There had been joking in the kitchen about the fly-papers when Bessie Brierley came down to the kitchen, and said there were some soaking in the bedroom, and joking going on between Alice Yapp and Alice Grant, the gardener's wife, about the Flannagan case, but they thought nothing about it, except as a joke. It was all done so openly, and certainly no thought entered their minds of suspecting Mrs. Maybrick about anything, until Michael Maybrick came into the house on the 8th May, and took control the way he did.

Alexander MacDougall.

Whatever Alice Yapp had dreamed up about the fly-papers and poisoning James's food had emanated from her visit to the kitchen that morning, and two hours later she had gone straight to Mrs. Briggs with her hot gossip.

Elizabeth Humphreys and Mary Cadwallader tell me what then occurred was this. That Mrs. Maybrick was sitting downstairs in the morning room with a lady friend, Mrs. Kennah, and had left the doors of the bedroom and sitting room open, so as to hear her husband if he wanted anything, and that Mrs. Briggs and Mrs. Hughes met Alice Yapp in the garden, and after some conversation, Alice Yapp brought them in by the back door and went up that way to the bedroom. Mrs. Maybrick, upon hearing them, went up to them and requested them to come downstairs. I know what

my wife would have done in the circumstances. I have no doubt she would have said to Mrs. Briggs and Mrs. Hughes all that Mrs. Maybrick said, and a great deal more.
                                                                    Alexander MacDougall.

Michael Maybrick's railway journey from London took five hours, but seemed interminable. No word had been received since sending the London medicine, other than James's letter incriminating Dr. Fuller, and the previous evening's telegram from Edwin. Anything could have been happening in Liverpool. Now, out of the blue, telegrams were flying around advising of James's deteriorating health, culminating in Mrs. Briggs mysterious message, 'Come at once. Strange things going on here.' James's illness had come as no surprise, as such was the intention, but how many people, if indeed any, had attributed this to the London medicine? Would Dr. Fuller be drawn in? The train seemed to be moving at walking pace.

When Michael eventually arrived in Liverpool, Edwin was waiting, and after updating Michael on James's deteriorating health, he recounted Alice Yapp's discovery of the fly-papers. This seemed too good to be true, and no mention of the London medicine. As soon as the brothers arrived at Battlecrease House, Edwin went to fetch Alice Yapp, who was only too willing to recount her tale, following which, at 10.30 p.m. that night, Michael made a special trip to Dr. Humphreys' house, to discuss not only James's condition, but the possible implications of Alice's discovery of the fly-papers. That same evening, undoubtedly on Michael's instructions, Edwin issued an edict to the nursing staff.

I gave orders on Wednesday night, and repeated them on Thursday evening. I never mentioned Mrs. Maybrick's name in the matter, but I told the nurses I should hold them responsible for all foods and medicines given to him, and that no-one was to attend him at all except the nurses, but did not mention any names. My orders would exclude Mrs. Maybrick and everybody else.

Edwin Maybrick.

Everybody that is, except Michael Maybrick, who had inadvertently stumbled upon a situation which just had to be exploited, immediately launching an unprovoked vendetta against Florence, accusing her of negligence in not caring for James, and holding her responsible for his deterioration.

I told her I had strong suspicions of the case. Then she asked me what I meant. I said that my suspicions were he had not been properly attended to, that he ought to have had a professional nurse and a second doctor earlier.

Michael Maybrick.

At no time did Edwin comment on Michael's unfounded accusations, despite having witnessed Florence's dedication to James over the last two weeks, and having personally organised, at Florence's insistence, the services of the highly respected Dr. Carter. Indeed, all indications are that James and Florence were once again happily reconciled. Florence soon heard of Edwin's presumptuous edict to the staff, and although undoubtedly distressed by his action, chose to ignore it, rightly assuming Michael had instigated the order. Nobody attempted to obstruct Florence's access to James, and her vigils continued as nurses Gore and Callery remained at James's side day and night. Following Michael's interventions, however, Nurse Gore's behaviour changed radically, and very soon she was given to regarding herself as nominally in charge of affairs.

The events of the morning of Thursday, 9th May are related by the cook, Elizabeth Humphreys, as Michael Maybrick began to make his presence known in Battlecrease House.

Mr. Michael Maybrick came to the house on Wednesday evening, the 8th May, late. On Thursday the 9th, I went up to the master's door early and met the mistress coming out. I went to the kitchen, and was followed shortly after by the mistress, who first ordered dinner, and then said 'Well, Humphreys, I am to blame for all this.' She seemed very much upset. On being asked in what way she was blamed, she said, 'For not getting proper nurses and other doctors.' She then walked away into the servants hall and there commenced to cry. She said she was very much put out, and added that her position in the house was not worth anything. She said that this is all through Michael Maybrick, that he had always had a spite against her since marriage. Mrs. Maybrick told me she had been turned out of the bedroom, and not allowed to give him his medicines. In speaking of Mr. Michael Maybrick, I remember that she said that if she went out of the house, he would not let her enter again.

Elizabeth Humphreys.

On Thursday, Michael and Edwin met with Alice Yapp to talk over her discovery at greater length, and, savouring the sweet taste of revenge, Alice then imparted her gossip regarding the fly-papers, just as she had to Mrs. Briggs earlier that day. Michael just couldn't believe his luck. This was indeed divine providence, that Florence could be suspected of poisoning James by arsenic, albeit in the fantasy world of children's nurse Alice Yapp. The Janion sisters too were deeply concerned at Alice's allegations regarding the fly-papers, remembering only too well the Flannagan case. Florence was not well-liked by the Janion sisters, and was detested by Alice, who would have been delighted to see

Florence divorced and destitute. The situation was beginning to look decidedly awkward for Florence, and Michael Maybrick decided to manipulate this to his advantage. Later that afternoon, Dr. Humphreys and Dr. Carter, unknown to each other before this series of events, were attending James when they were confronted by an officious Michael Maybrick. Dr. Carter recalls the meeting,

At 4.30 on Thursday, the 9th, I went out in response to a telegram, and then for the first time saw Mr. Michael Maybrick. 'Now what is the matter with my brother, Dr. Carter?' was a question put to me very abruptly, in the presence of Dr. Humphreys. I repeated the opinion we had formed. 'But what is the cause of it?' was the next question, as abruptly put as the first. 'That is by no means clear to us,' I replied, 'It may have been caused by many things. The conclusion we formed was that your brother must have committed a grave error of diet, by taking some irritant food or drink, or both, and so have set up inflammation.' Turning then sharply to Dr. Humphreys, Michael Maybrick asked him if he had informed me of the subject of their last night's conversation. Dr. Humphreys simply replied that he had informed me of nothing. All this was a matter of grave surprise to me. I did not know until that moment that any conversation had taken place, and as I had had no communication with Dr. Humphreys, I looked at the speaker wondering what would come next. 'God forbid that I should unjustly suspect anyone', he said, 'but do you not think if I have serious grounds for fearing that all may not be right, that it is my duty to say so to you?' We thought that it was. We heard that only so late as the middle of April, the patient had not been able to eat any ordinary food at his house, that he had soon been subject to sick attacks after returning home, that this contrast between the condition of health, while away and at home respectively, had been the subject of remark, and it had been noticed before that there was a most serious

estrangement between the husband and the wife, that the wife was known to be unfaithful, and that just before the commencement of illness, she was known to have procured many fly-papers, and having heard all this, we consulted together, and we stated clearly what we conceived to be our own duty under the painful circumstances.
                                                    Dr. William Carter.

The doctors, although astute and intelligent, were no match for Michael Maybrick's duplicity, and soon found themselves concurring with his assertions of foul play. The plan was now under way to deflect attention away from the London medicine, and concentrate on the fly-papers, which Alice Yapp had unwittingly introduced as cause to suspect Florence of foul play. Michael was pulling the strings, planting suspicion, but taking great care to remain in the background, leaving others to draw their own conclusions. A dangerous scenario was slowly unfolding into which Florence Maybrick was about to be drawn. Life would never be the same again.

COUNTDOWN

James Maybrick's health continued to deteriorate, and Michael Maybrick next proceeded to put into operation a plan which involved the unwitting participation of the austere Nurse Ellen Gore, who would now be held personally responsible for the patient's well-being, a position of authority to which the nurse readily acceded. Nurse Gore relates the introduction of a new bottle of Valentine's Meat Juice, personally handed to her by Edwin on the evening of Michael's arrival at Battlecrease House.

Nurse Callery remained in charge until I returned at eleven o' clock on the night of Thursday the 9th. I obtained a bottle of Valentine's Meat Juice from the landing. It appeared to be unopened and perfectly new. I had seen the bottle before. I have no reason to think the bottle had been tampered with. Mr. Edwin Maybrick gave it to me the night (Wednesday) previously. I tasted it to see if it was alright. I gave Mr. Maybrick two teaspoonsful in water. Mrs. Maybrick was present. She said Mr. Maybrick had had Valentine's Meat Juice before and it had made him sick.

Nurse Gore.

Edwin was clearly acting on Michael's instructions, as was Nurse Gore when she inexplicably 'tasted it to see if it was alright.' Why? On no other occasion had Edwin been involved in prescribing James's medicines, nor is there mention of any of the nurses pre-tasting medicine, like food tasters at the court of Lucrezia Borgia. Both were following specific instructions from the self-assumed master of Battlecrease House, for whom this carefully monitored bottle of Valentine's Meat Juice was to be an integral factor in the ongoing scheme to destroy Florence, who was about to compound her already delicate situation by inadvertently arousing the suspicions of Nurse Gore.

After midnight I gave him Champagne, and he went to sleep for three quarters of an hour. Mrs. Maybrick was in the room during that time. A few minutes after twelve o'clock, Mrs. Maybrick, in passing to the dressing room, picked up the bottle of Valentine's Meat Juice from the table, and took it into the dressing room and closed the door. She remained about two minutes. Then she came back and stood by the small window table, and told me to get some ice to put into the water to bathe Mr. Maybrick's head. I said the patient was sleeping, and I would do it when he awoke. Whilst she was talking to me, she put the bottle of meat juice back on the table. She appeared to be trying to conceal her action from my view.

Nurse Gore.

Florence, by her own admission, had added a white powder to the meat juice at James's insistence, which could well have been James's prescription mixture from Clay and Abrahams, but which was never subsequently identified, as it is on record that Nurse Gore threw the mixture down the sink, intent on ensuring that the liquid never reached James's lips. Florence had played straight into Michael's hands by handling the bottle. Had Nurse Gore been instructed to allow Florence to have a free hand that evening, as indeed she was used to doing, with no malicious intent whatsoever?

I was overwrought, terribly anxious, miserably unhappy, and his evident distress utterly unnerved me. He had told me the powder would not harm him, and I could put it in his food.

Florence Maybrick.

Nurse Gore would later confirm that she instructed Nurse Callery, on duty the following day, to guard the bottle carefully, and to take a sample from the bottle in the course of her watch. Why do this, when she was perfectly capable of taking the sample herself? Nurse Gore was simply following orders, securing another independent witness to affirm the bottle's provenance. Michael knew full well that Florence was not poisoning James, and his plan was to switch the guarded bottle during Nurse Callery's ensuing afternoon watch, prior to the sample being taken, for a bottle containing 'a little something he had prepared earlier.' Nurse Callery, as per Nurse Gore's instructions, was to take the sample from Michael's doctored bottle for eventual presentation to Dr. Carter, who, after analysis, would discover an arsenic content. Both nurses would confirm having monitored the newly opened bottle to the point when the sample would be taken, ensuring three impartial witnesses, including Edwin, to the provenance of the bottle, with of course, no involvement whatsoever by Michael Maybrick. Florence would be the only suspect. However, all did not go to plan.

When Michael entered James's bedroom around noon the following day, intending to surreptitiously switch the bottles prior to the sample being taken, much to his surprise Nurse Callery had already bottled and sealed a sample. There follows a very strange sequence of events. Nurse Callery, totally oblivious of all that was happening, relates,

On Friday the 10th, I was on duty from 11 a.m. till 4.30 p.m. Nurse Gore said something to me. My attention was called by her to a bottle of Valentine's Meat Juice which was on the table in Mr. Maybrick's room. I took a sample out of the meat juice, and put it into an ordinary medicine bottle. I took the sample because I was asked to do so by Nurse Gore. I threw the sample away on Nurse Gore's coming from the Nurses Home on Friday at 2.00 p.m., because Nurse Gore had been to the Lady Superintendent, and she had requested Nurse Gore not to take a sample.

This is all very strange. No query appears to have been raised as to why the Lady Superintendent, based miles away in the Nurses' Institute, would have been approached or would have issued such an instruction. More likely Nurse Gore had been confronted by a furious Michael Maybrick, asserting an error of judgment by the nurses, and proffering the assertion that he had cleared the matter with the Lady Superintendent? A complete fabrication, made in the knowledge that neither Nurse Gore or Nurse Callery would dream of confirming this with their formidable headmistress, who, in reality, would have been totally unaware of the strange events unfolding at Battlecrease House. Author J.H. Levy, writing ten years later in 1899, makes the following observation.

At the Coroner's inquest, Nurse Callery swore that when Nurse Gore asked her to throw away the sample of the meat juice that had been taken, she said that the Lady Superintendent at the Nurse's Institute had given directions to that effect. This lady is since dead, but Mr. MacDougall states that she informed him that she never gave any such direction. Nurse Gore does not appear to have sworn that she did so.

With his master plan unravelling, and having blustered his way through that unexpected hurdle, the only course of action left was for Michael to take possession of the bottle from Nurse Callery and substitute it with his own. Where, incidentally, had he obtained the substitute bottle? One of the servants, Bessie Brierley may have the answer.

On Thursday, the 9th of May, I went to my master's bedroom, and as I got to the bedroom door I met Mrs. Maybrick coming out. I remember taking a cup of tea into the mistress's bedroom. It was the front room I took it into. As I

passed through the chamber, Mr. Maybrick was in bed, and the nurse was rubbing his hands. When I passed through on returning, Mr. Michael Maybrick was in the room, and I saw him take something off the wash-stand. This occurred on the Thursday evening.
Bessie Brierley.

Personal involvement in the bottle's provenance was totally contrary to the plan, but now Michael had no alternative, so when Dr. Carter and Dr. Humphreys arrived at 4.30 p.m., Michael presented them with his suitably doctored substitute bottle of Valentine's Meat Juice. The doctors had absolutely no reason to suspect the provenance of the bottle, and Dr. Carter confirmed that he would take the necessary steps, as soon as possible, to have the contents analysed. Florence Maybrick, writing years later, leaves no doubt that mischief was afoot.

Mr. Edwin Maybrick took it upon himself to procure a fresh bottle, and, distinctly against the doctor's orders, Nurse Gore set about to administer its contents .... I say it is absolutely clear that the bottle of Valentine's Meat Juice which Mr. Michael Maybrick took possession of and handed to Dr. Carter, is not the same bottle which Nurse Gore saw me place on the washstand. There should be no flaw in the identity of the bottle which was handed to an analyst and the one which was in my hands.
Mrs. Maybrick's Own Story.
Florence Maybrick.

J.H. Levy continues with more very pertinent observations.

It may be remarked as a curious fact in the case that Nurse Callery, though cautioned to keep a close eye on the bottle of meat juice, did not see Mr. Michael Maybrick remove it, nor did she miss it during the remainder of her watch. Was it a different bottle he took away?
J.H. Levy.

After Dr. Carter had taken possession of the bottle, the doctors then went upstairs to continue their treatment, which in itself makes quite startling reading.

In the afternoon, the patient's pulse was still more rapid, and one of his hands was becoming white. Generally, he was weaker and decidedly worse. I ordered some sulphoral for his restlessness, nitro-glycerine for his hand, cocaine for his throat, and also some phosphoric acid for his mouth.
Dr. Humphreys.

Michael Maybrick may just as well have let the doctors finish him off. Arsenic may have provided light relief after phosphoric acid. Dr. Carter then added even more to the cocktails already provided,

On Friday, the 10th, we suggested a nutrient suppository, if it could be retained, some sulphoral, and one nitro glycerine tablet. He was also taking brandy and Champagne.
Dr. William Carter.

Why not tincture of dynamite suppository? Was Nurse Gore still on tasting duty, one wonders? Unsurprisingly, James's condition continued to deteriorate. An American physician Dr. Helen Densmore, who later took an active interest in the Maybrick saga, had no hesitation in apportioning blame for James's deterioration.

Anxious, no doubt, to do the best they could for their patient, sincerely believing with great faith in the efficacy of the doses they prescribed, they gave him the following. Bismuth. Sulphoral. Cocaine. Nitro-Glycerine. Phosphoric Acid. Cascara. Nitro Hydrochloric Acid. Plummer's Pills, containing Antimony and Calomel. Prussic Acid. Bromide of Potassium. Tincture of Hyoscyamus. Tincture of Henbane. Antipyrine. Papaine's Iridine. Jabourandi. Chlorine. Morphia. Fowler's Solution of Arsenic. Bismuth and Opium. Now, here are upwards of twenty different medical drugs,

most of them deadly poisons, given to this poor patient by his medical advisers. What does it read like? Is it not an insult to common sense? Will it not be read like a burlesque on the medical science of the present enlightened age? Is there a man who dares to assert that if the above list of deadly poisons were given to a patient during an illness, he would not be injured thereby? How could it expected otherwise?
The Maybrick Case. Dr. Helen Densmore. 1892.

The next strange sequence of events involved the will supposedly signed by James in the last moments of his life, and eventually lodged in Somerset House.

Soon after handing over the adulterated bottle to the doctors, Michael had stepped up the game to the next level. By late afternoon of Friday, 10th May, it was evident to all that James Maybrick was a dying man. Time was running out, James must not be allowed to recover, and certain matters required attention before the master plan could be put into operation. Barrister Alexander MacDougall, writing in 1891, and deeply cynical of the goings-on at Battlecrease House, relates the unfolding events,

On that Friday evening, at about seven o'clock, a rather remarkable thing occurred, which must not be kept back, and must be thoroughly investigated. I shall give the description of that occurrence as it has been supplied to me by two of the servants, Elizabeth Humphreys, the cook, and Mary Cadwallader, the parlour-maid. The office clerks, Thomas Lowry and George Smith, came up to the house with some papers. Michael and Edwin Maybrick were there, and took them to James Maybrick. After some time, James started shouting at the brothers in a loud voice that could be heard all over the house. 'Oh Lord, if I am to die, why am I to be worried by this? Let me die properly.' He was very violent, and shouted out very loud. Both Humphreys and

Cadwallader saw Edwin come out of the bedroom with a paper in his hand, and they say that Alice Yapp, whom they describe as, 'knowing and hearing everything', told them that they had been trying to get him to sign the will, and after the day of the quarrel on the day of the Grand National, James Maybrick had made a new will, and Michael and Edwin could not find it, and they were trying to get one signed.

Alexander MacDougall.

According to Alice, a will, formulated on the day after the Grand National, the 29th March 1889, could not be found, if indeed one ever existed. The only will in existence, lodged in Somerset House, was dated the 25th April, and reads as follows,

In case I die before having made a regular proper Will in legal form, I wish this to be taken as my last Will and Testament. I leave and bequeath all my worldly possessions of whatever kind or description, including furniture, pictures, wines, linen, plate, life insurances, cash, shares, property, in fact everything I possess, in trust with my brothers Michael Maybrick and Thomas Maybrick, for my two children James Chandler Maybrick and Gladys Eveleyn Maybrick. The furniture I desire to remain intact, and to be used in furnishing a home which can be shared by my widow and children but the furniture to be the children's. I further desire that all moneys be invested in the name of the above trustees (Michael and Thomas Maybrick) and the income of same used for the children's benefit and education, said education to be left to the discretion of the said trustees.

My widow will have for her portion of my estate the policies on my life, say £500 with the Scottish Widows Fund and £2,000 with the Mutual Reserve Fund Life Association of New York both policies being made out in her name. The interest on this £2,500 together with the £125 a year which she receives from her New York property will make a provision of about £125 a year, a sum although small, will yet be the means of keeping her respectably.

It is also my desire that my widow shall live under the same roof as the children so long as she remains my widow. If it is legally possible I wish the £2,500 of Life Insurance on my life in my wife's name to be invested in the names of said Trustees, but that she should have the sole use of the interest thereof during her lifetime, but at her death, the principle revert to my said children James Chandler and Gladys Eveleyn Maybrick. Witness my hand and seal this twenty fifth day of April 1889.

Signed James Maybrick.

Signed by the Testator in the presence of us who at his request in his presence and the presence of each other have hereunto affixed our names as witnesses,

George R. Davidson and George Smith.

The will was purportedly written by James Maybrick, yet on the two occasions when his daughter's name occurs, Evelyn is mis-spelled 'Eveleyn', hardly a mistake to be made twice by her loving father, whatever his state of mind, and especially considering there are no other spelling errors in the will. Also within the will is an obvious error in computing the interest payable on the life policies, plus Florence's own £125, purportedly still only totalling £125 per annum. Initially, everything, including life policies, is left in trust to Michael and Thomas; then Florence is granted the life policies, but with an incorrectly computed annuity of only £125; then the capital value of the policies is once again invested in the Trustees. The format is ambiguous and contradictory, and the will was clearly prepared without legal advice. The result of this bizarre arrangement, if uncontested, would effectively leave Michael in total control of affairs, with Thomas the token gesture to shared responsibility. Florence would receive less than three pounds a week, and the children's education and welfare would be dependent upon, of all people, Michael Maybrick. Is this really what James would have intended? More importantly, was this will the genuine article, or was it the work of a man intent on the downfall of Florence Maybrick, and indeed James?

The document is written on two pages, bearing two neat signatures, which are certainly not the scrawl of a semi-conscious man on his deathbed. By Michael's own admission, James was delirious by 6 o'clock.

From 2 o'clock, my brother grew gradually worse, and by 6 o'clock, he was highly delirious.

A new will, presented to a dying, delirious man for signature, has very sinister overtones indeed. Something very irregular was taking place on that fateful evening of Friday, 10th May, in which Edwin was complicit, and which, at the very least, casts doubts as to the authenticity of the will which was eventually lodged in Somerset House.

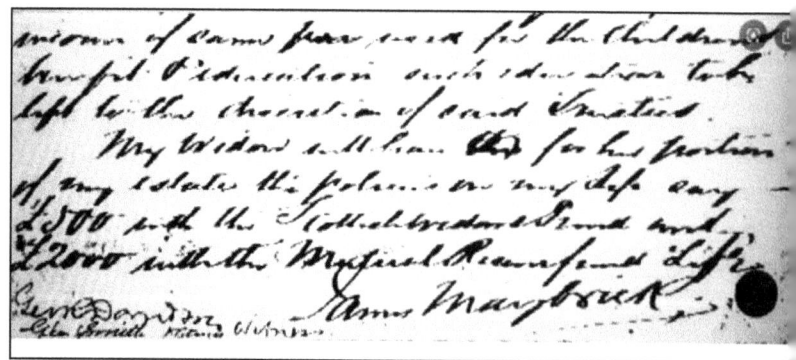

Will of James Maybrick lodged at Somerset House. Page 1.

Will of James Maybrick, lodged at Somerset House. Page 2.

Author Shirley Harrison, in 'The Diary of Jack the Ripper', commissioned document analyst and handwriting expert Susan Iremonger, Member of the World Association of Document Examiners, who made the following observations.

I cannot, however, get away from the fact that both James and Michael have incredibly similar writing. Even taking into account their parallel schooling, I would not have expected to find such a similar style and weight of strokes.

Diary of Jack the Ripper. Shirley Harrison.

Signatures, however, are an entirely different matter, individually honed over the years. Herewith are hitherto unseen examples, from Masonic archives, of James Maybrick's signature, underlined by a unique characteristic flourish, unlike the signatures in the will. All indications are that this will was the work of Michael Maybrick. The document was dated the 24th April, the day after the Grand Lodge Investiture, and three days after Dr. Fuller's discovery of Michael having provided James with strychnine based pills. It was also the date when the London Medicine was posted to Battlecrease House. What had prompted these actions? This was the same calculating mindset which had orchestrated the murder of selected victims in Whitechapel according to a carefully contrived stategy, just as the strychnine pills, the will, and the London Medicine were to form part of another pre-conceived plan, only this time the victims were to be James and Florence Maybrick, to be silenced in entirely different ways.

The clock was ticking on that fateful evening of the

10th May, and the signatures of witnesses George Davidson and George Smith were urgently required to validate the document prior to James's imminent demise. James's office clerk, George Smith, would have done as instructed by Michael Maybrick, but James's closest friend George Davidson may well have been uncomfortable with the content of the will, and the fact that he was not actually witnessing James signing the document, already dated a fortnight earlier. Perhaps also, as a working colleague, he was familiar with James's signature. Was he actually afforded the opportunity of reading the will, or brusquely asked for his signature at the bottom of the page? Did a dispute arise, causing James to cry out 'Lord, if I am to die, why am I to be worried by this?' George Davidson decided to accede to the request, but was beginning to harbour doubts, and not without justification.

R.I.P.

Alice Yapp, the lowly children's nurse with lofty self-esteem, had proved a most unexpected ally to Michael Maybrick, sharing with him a burning hatred of Florence, and a devious mindset which could be put to good use. Despite the vivid images of Mary Jane Kelly flashing through his mind, cutting Florence's throat was definitely out of the question, so character assassination would have to suffice, leading to a charge of murder by poison if all went to plan. A solution had to be found, quickly, and Alice Yapp would prove to be a willing accomplice.

On the morning of Saturday, 11th May, three days after Michael's arrival, Florence succumbed to what was described as a 'speechless swoon', and was carried by Edwin from James's bedroom into a spare room, where she remained in that condition until Monday. No explanation has been given for this mysterious occurrence, but Edwin later provides an indication of Florence's unusual symptoms.

As far as I am aware, she did not exactly faint. We spoke to her several times, but she did not reply. She seemed to be in a semi-conscious state, or partially asleep, I do not know which.

Opium based laudanum was a drug readily available from any apothecary's shop, but too difficult to administer unknowingly, and the effects would not have been as long-lasting as were Florence's symptoms. Hypnosis, however, was practiced scientifically at the time, as well as appearing to excited reviews on the Victorian theatre circuit, where the famous Michael Maybrick also performed. Was Florence particularly susceptible to hypnotic induction, as indicated by

Edwin's description of her condition? Whatever the cause of the mysterious 'swoon' no comment seems to have been forthcoming from any of the doctors in the house over that fateful weekend. On Saturday, Dr. Carter and Dr. Humphreys convened to discuss with Michael Maybrick the analysis of the Valentine's Meat Juice, which he had obligingly handed over the day before. Dr. Carter produced copper test strips coated with a metallic deposit, indicative of an alien substance, taking great care to make no specific reference to arsenic, pending submission to a specialist for more intrusive tests. The doctors remained on hand for the rest of the day, whilst, in the meantime, Michael instructed his team of willing helpers, Alice Yapp and the Janion sisters, to set about exploring the house for the missing will, totally unaccountable to anyone, with both James and Florence incapacitated. No cupboard or drawer was left unsearched, and suspect items were exposed, but left untouched. Given Alice Yapp's disposition to pry into her employers' affairs, was she already aware of James's 'secret' stache of powders, which had arrived earlier in the year? Armed with this confidential information, did Michael plan to strategically re-distribute the items prior to a planned 'discovery', in front of witnesses?

At 8.40 p.m., on Saturday, 11th May, James Maybrick took his last breath, in the arms of his dear friend, George Davidson. The doctors went on their way, Dr. Carter taking with him Michael Maybrick's incriminating bottle of Valentine's Meat Juice, which he delivered to Mr. Edward Davies, Fellow of the Pharmaceutical Society, for further analysis. The way was now clear for the search party to head straight for their earlier finds, relishing the excitement of pleasing their new overlord. The indefatigable Alexander MacDougall adds his touch to what happened next.

As soon as the breath was out of the body of James Maybrick, and while the widow was lying in this mysterious speechless swoon, Michael and Edwin Maybrick, Mrs. Briggs and Mrs. Hughes usurped control in the house, sent the children away, and, together with Alice Yapp went straight to places open and accessible to everybody, and put their hands, without any difficulty, upon large quantities of arsenic in all sorts of forms, arsenic mixed with charcoal, 'poison for cats', bottles of arsenic in crystals, enough altogether to poison fifty people, and a remarkable circumstance in connection with these things is that, although these five people found this arsenic in places open and accessible to everybody, nobody had seen any of it in the house before, and nobody could say where it had all come from.

Alexander MacDougall.

These would certainly appear to be part of James Maybrick's secret supply of black and white arsenic, acquired from Valentine Blake in January. Alice Yapp made the first official discovery on the Saturday, inside a trunk which she had earlier manhandled into the children's nursery, assisted by Betty Brierley. In the presence of independent witness Nurse Wilson, Alice exhibited the contents, including a package marked 'Arsenic for Cats', to a theatrically surprised Michael Maybrick, who instructed Edwin to summon an even more reliable witness, next door neighbour, barrister and England cricketer, Douglas Steel, to substantiate the find. The lawyer suggested the items be locked in the cellar, and Michael complied, pocketing the key. Further suspect items, including a number of bottles, were found on Sunday by Matilda Briggs, in a prominent position in the room off James's bedroom.

Nobody at Battlecrease House was prepared to concede that James was an arsenic addict. Florence was to be portrayed as his murderer, and the newly discovered items were to be construed as incriminating evidence. At the same time as this scenario was unfolding, Michael and Edwin were on a mission of their own, in a frantic search for James's April will. Florence was still semi-comatose, only vaguely aware of the events unfolding around her.

Slowly consciousness returned. The room was in darkness. All was still. Suddenly the silence was broken by the bang of a closing door which started me out of my stupor. Where was I? Why was I alone? What awful thing had happened? A flash of memory. My husband was dead! I drifted once more away from the things of sense. Then a voice, as if a long way off spoke. Edwin Maybrick was bending over me as I lay upon my bed. He had my arms tightly gripped, and was shaking me violently. 'I want your keys, - do you hear? Where are your keys?' he exclaimed harshly. I tried to form a reply, but the words choked me, and once more I passed into unconsciousness.

It is the dawn of a Sabbath day. I am still lying in my clothes, neglected and uncared for, without food since the morning of the day before. Consciousness came and went. During one of these intervals, Michael Maybrick entered. 'Nurse', he said, 'I am going to London. Mrs. Maybrick is no longer mistress of this house. As one of the executors, I forbid you to allow her to leave this room. I hold you responsible in my absence.' He then left the room. What did he mean? How dare he humble me thus in the presence of a stranger. Towards the night of the same day, I said to the nurse, 'I wish to see my children.' She took no notice. My voice was weak, and I thought perhaps she had not heard. 'Nurse,' I repeated, 'I want to see my children' She walked up to my bed, and in a cold, deliberate voice replied, 'You cannot see Master James and Miss Gladys. Mr. Michael Maybrick gave orders that they were to leave the house without seeing you.' I fell back on my pillow, dazed and stricken, weak, helpless and impotent. Why was I treated thus?

Mrs. Maybrick's Story. Florence Maybrick.

On the morning of Monday 13th May, Dr. Humphreys, much influenced by the intervention of Michael Maybrick on the Friday evening, decided that as arsenic had been found on the premises, he was unable to issue a Death Certificate, and reported the matter to the local Coroner, who ordered a post mortem. At 5 pm, whilst Florence was still lying in bed, tended by the nurses, Dr. Humphreys and Dr. Carter arrived to carry out a post-mortem on James's corpse, bringing with them Dr. Alexander Barron, pathologist at Liverpool Royal Infirmary. Parts of the stomach, liver and intestines were removed, placed in jars and taken away for analysis. On being routinely notified by the Coroner of the doctor's refusal of a Death Certificate, Superintendent Isaac Bryning of the Garston Constabulary immediately made his way to Battlecrease House.

The first encounter between Michael Maybrick and Superintendent Bryning is not documented, and whilst each was a powerful character, the formidable police officer, with twenty five years' service on the tough streets of Liverpool, was no match for Michael Maybrick. The Superintendent would have listened attentively as Michael Maybrick, in stentorian tones, demanded justice for his poor dead brother, poisoned by a scheming adulterous wife. James was indeed Michael's brother, and, as he now discovered, so was Brother Isaac Bryning of the Lodge of Harmony No.220, meeting at the Garston Hotel, Liverpool. The Inspector had only been a Freemason for five years, and would have been in awe of

Brother Michael Maybrick, Acting Grand Officer, London, personal acquaintance of the Grand Master HRH The Prince of Wales, and the Deputy Grand Master, Lord Lathom, Lord Chamberlain, Provincial Grand Master of Lancashire, and fellow Lodge member of Michael's deceased brother James in St. George's Lodge of Harmony, No.32, meeting at the Adelphi Hotel, Liverpool. The brethren of the Garston Hotel, in common with all Lodges in England, toasted these icons at every Lodge meeting.

Before the Superintendent left, Edwin Maybrick joined the pair and handed over the bottles which had been discovered, but retaining the 'Arsenic for Cats' found by Alice Yapp, and still locked in the cellar, the key to which was held by Michael Maybrick. Superintendent Bryning's official version of the evening's events was 'I made enquiries, and took particulars.' No further details were ever ascertained, but let there be no doubt as to who provided the 'particulars', none of which have ever been released for public scrutiny. No police officers were summoned to cordon the premises, no application made for a search warrant, and everyone was left free to wander around the house, with evidence left totally unattended. Brother Michael Maybrick was firmly in charge of investigations at Battlecrease House, and Florence was in serious trouble.

The Superintendent returned to Battlecrease House later that afternoon, accompanied by Inspector Richard Baxendale, who interviewed the servants, including the effusive Alice Yapp, and also supervised inspection of the drains, whilst Dr. Humphreys collected sediment samples for analysis. Michael Maybrick enjoined the police officers in conversation, discovering to his undisguised delight that Brother Richard

Baxendale was also a member of the Lodge of Harmony, Garston, initiated in 1883, one year before Brother Isaac Bryning. There is no record of how long this convivial meeting lasted, or how many brandies were consumed, as the Liverpool police officers were regaled by tales of Brother Maybrick's royal and social contacts in London, leading eventually and inevitably to the indisputable fact of Florence's guilt, with total reliance on these splendid officers to ensure the wicked murderess would not escape justice whilst matters were under their jurisdiction. At the conclusion of this affable evening, Michael Maybrick handed over the package marked 'Arsenic for Cats', retained in the cellar for the past two days, under his personal custody, as obvious evidence of Florence's murderous intentions. Interestingly, Florence owned three cats, one of which was her constant companion, rendering it farcical that Florence would have contrived such a package as 'Arsenic for Cats.'

The conduct of the police, in conjunction with those conspiring against Mrs. Maybrick at the time of the event, aptly illustrates the pernicious system of police regulations. The clues were given to them, none were discovered by them. The evidence shows, for example, that large quantities of arsenic were found in the house after Mr. Maybrick's death. Not a grain, however, was found in any secret locked up place, and not one grain of the arsenic was ever traced to Mrs. Maybrick, nor was it found before Mr. Maybrick's death, but was shown to the police afterwards. Upon this prepared line of discovery, an abnormal activity was at once developed. It was quite clear that no portion of the arsenic was used by Mrs. Maybrick to poison her husband, and if the police could discover this suspiciously large quantity of arsenic, enough to kill fifty persons, their activity, it would seem, might also furnish a valuable clue to the real criminal in this abhorrent and unnatural combination to destroy an innocent woman.

The Maybrick Case. Dr. Helen Densmore. 1892.

On Wednesday, 15th May, a report appeared in the Liverpool Daily Post, under the headline 'Suspicious Death of Liverpool Merchant', a mere morsel compared to the feast of innuendos which were about to follow over the next few weeks, but the intrigue had begun.

Michael Maybrick wasted no time in putting Mrs. Briggs in charge of affairs at Battlecrease House, whilst blending into the background, well away from the consequences of his chicanery. This did not go un-noticed amongst James's friends, including Charles Ratcliffe.

Old Humphries made a jackass of himself. After James died, he and Dr. Carter expected to make out the Death Certificate as acute inflammation of the stomach. After Humphreys had a conversation with Michael he refused to make a certificate to that effect, but said there were strong symptoms of arsenical poisoning, though Dr. Carter insisted that it should be inflammation of the stomach. Now wouldn't that cork you? A musical composer instructing a physician how to diagnose his case. Michael, the son of a bitch, should have his throat cut. When Michael took possession and put Mrs. Briggs in charge, Florence was subjected to all kinds of insults and ill-treatment by Briggs and the servants. She was not allowed any visits from her friends. She was cursed and given impudent answers whenever she made a request of them.

Letters from Charles Ratcliffe to John Aunspaugh. 7 June 1889.

In the course of the following few days, a stream of well-meaning friends and acquaintances of the Maybricks called at Battlecrease House to express their condolences, all of whom were turned away by Matilda Briggs, explaining that

Florence was grieving in bed, unable to entertain visitors, whilst in reality ensuring that Florence was on her own, friendless, with no-one to offer so much as a word of comfort.

Mrs. Maybrick was at once arrested and placed under guard in her own room. No-one knew anything about this. Michael then took possession of Battlecrease, and put Mrs. Briggs in charge. My wife and myself called, and were told by Mrs. Briggs that Mrs. Maybrick was too sick to receive any company. Sutton and his wife called, Holloway and his wife, Hienes and his wife, and numerous others. They were all told the same thing. No-one could see Mrs. Maybrick.

Letters from Charles Ratcliffe to John Aunspaugh. 7 June 1889.

BARONESS VON ROQUES

Michael Maybrick was pompous, disdainful and overwhelmingly assertive, and since his arrival in Liverpool, everyone, without exception, had been skilfully coerced by this master of manipulation. No difficulty had been experienced in taking control of Battlecrease House and recruiting his team of sycophantic helpers, whilst the level-headed doctors, Carter and Humphreys, had been readily persuaded by the unqualified suggestion of arsenic poisoning, on which the masterplan depended. Superintendent Bryning and Inspector Baxendale, deferring to Michael Maybrick's superior Masonic credentials, had been flattered to be embraced as equals by the great man, and were resolutely determined to secure by any means the conviction of the evil woman who had murdered his brother.

The inquest was fixed for the 14th May at the Aigburth Hotel, Garston. Prior to the meeting, 39 year old Coroner Samuel Brighouse had been pleasantly surprised to be warmly embraced by Mr. Michael Maybrick, and was immediately captivated by the sincerity of this upright pillar of the establishment, rightly aggrieved at the death of his brother, in circumstances already explained in great detail by the Coroner's long-standing court associate of four years standing, Superintendent Isaac Bryning. When Michael Maybrick expressed apprehension that a just outcome may be perverted by the introduction of clever legal technicalities, the message was not lost on the impartial Coroner Brighouse, who had by now decided on the outcome of proceedings. This was his court, and no such occurrence would occur.

The inquest was duly opened, and the jury of fourteen men sworn in, following which all present journeyed to Battlecrease House, where Michael Maybrick formally identified the body. The hearing was then adjourned for a fortnight, pending analysis of body parts taken at the post-mortem, and, after medical assurances from Dr. Humphreys, the party then crowded into Florence's bedroom, listening attentively to the words of Superintendent Bryning,

Mrs. Maybrick, I am Superintendent of the Police, and I am about to say something to you. After I have said what I intend to say, if you reply, be careful how you reply, because whatever you say may be used as evidence against you. Mrs. Maybrick, you are in custody on causing the death of your late husband, James Maybrick on the eleventh instant.

Mrs. Maybrick's Story. Florence Maybrick.

On the advice of the officials present, Michael notified Florence of the need for legal representation, and, on Dr. Humphreys' recommendation, a telegram was despatched to solicitors Richard and Arnold Cleaver, who at once made their way to Battlecrease House, only to receive minimal information from their client, who had been in bed for the last four days, totally unaware of the proceedings unfolding about her. Freemason Richard Cleaver, of Mount Lebanon Lodge No.216, doubtless received a more detailed and suitably biased version of events from Bros. Maybrick, Bryning and Baxendale. Shortly afterwards, Bro. Cleaver was approached by Bro. John Dalglish, foreman of the jury, fellow member of the same Lodge as the police officers, and a Masonic colleague of the late Bro. James Maybrick. Bro. Dalglish explained that, whilst at the Wirral Races, he had witnessed James taking a white powder, which he confessed was strychnine. He was not the only person to have witnessed

James's intake that day, as the same tale had already been recounted by fellow punter William Thomson, further endorsed by family acquaintances, Mr. and Mrs. Morden Rigg. As John Dalglish's information was considered to be relevant to the cause of death, Richard Cleaver resolved to raise the matter when the inquest was re-convened.

On the morning of Thursday 6th May, the funeral cortège arrived at Battlecrease House, where Florence was allowed a few minutes with the coffin before it was carried into the hearse, which was followed by a retinue of nine cabs on the journey to Anfield Cemetery, where a waiting crowd watched as the coffin was lowered into the ground. Florence was now a prisoner in her bedroom at Battlecrease House, with a resident bedside nurse and a policeman on either side of the door. On enquiring why her mother was not present, no response was forthcoming from anyone, but later that afternoon Michael sent a telegram to the Baroness in Paris, stating 'Florie ill and in awful trouble. Do not delay.' The Baroness left Paris immediately, and made her way to Liverpool.

I arrived from Paris at Liverpool on Friday, 17th of May. I met Michael Maybrick by chance in the station at Liverpool, where he said to me, 'Florie is very ill, Edwin will tell you everything. It is a case of murder, and there is a man in the case.' Not comprehending at all, and perfectly dazed, I went out to Battlecrease House. I had never been there before. Edwin met me in the vestibule, and took me into the morning room. He was much agitated. I asked what it all meant, and said, 'Why did you not send for me before, why was I not allowed to come?' He said, 'Florie did not ask for you, and no one knew your address.' I said, 'Oh, everyone knew it. Paris would have found me. Tell me what happened, Michael told me you would explain. I must see Florie at once.' He replied, 'The police are in the house.' I said, 'Police, why?' He replied, 'I suppose you know it is said Jim was poisoned.' I asked, 'Poisoned by whom?' Then he went on to tell me in a broken way that Michael had suspected, and the doctor thought something was wrong. I said, 'What doctor?' He replied, 'Dr. Carter, and we thought Jim was not properly nursed. The nurse said Florie put something in the meat juice, and Michael gave it to Dr. Carter.' I said ''Why not have sent for me? How could you deliver her up to the police in this way, and not a friend by her. Who has been here?' He said, 'Mrs. Briggs, but she left on Wednesday. I assure you that we had no idea matters would result in this way. I would rather cut my hand off than have it so.' 'I said, 'But the children. How could you ruin their future? Your suspicions alone are horrible, and for a girl like that, without father, brother, mother. You are doing her to death among you, and for what motive?' 'Oh!' he exclaimed, 'I have been very fond of Florie. I would never have believed wrong of her. I would have stood by her, and I did until the letter to a man was found.' I said. 'Letter to a man, what man? Do, Edwin, tell me a straight story.' He replied, 'Why, to the man Brierley. She wrote him a letter, and it was found.' I said, 'Who found it? You? And who is Brierley? When did she know him? She never mentioned him to me?' He replied, 'She met him this winter at some dances, and she was always so quiet and domestic before. I would have never believed it of Florie, but this winter she was changed, and would go out to dances. I wish I could meet Brierley.' 'Yes,' I exclaimed, 'that is just about the best thing you could do. In my country and among the men I have known, they would have met Brierley, instead of calling in the police. But about this letter? Who found it?' He said, 'Nurse.' I asked, 'Where? and if she found it, why did she not give it back to her mistress? What have you to do with it?' He replied, 'She found it on the floor, it fell from her dress when she fainted, and I carried her into the spare *bedroom.'* But I said, *'How did you know it was to Brierley?'* He replied, *'It was directed to him, it was written in pencil and it fell to the floor.' 'I was in despair at this disconnected story, and went upstairs.'*

This letter, henceforth to be referred to as the 'Brierley Letter', was to be of pivotal importance in the life of Florence Elizabeth Maybrick. Disconnected as the story was regarding the discovery of the letter, blurted out by Edwin on the spur of the moment with his mind in turmoil, it certainly appears honest and uncontrived. James's death, Florence's 'swoon', and the discovery of the letter, all occurred on Saturday 11th May, three days after Michael's arrival. The Baroness continues,

I found two policemen in the hall upstairs. I went in through an open door, my daughter was lying on the sofa, deadly pale, a policeman was sitting on a chair near the sofa (I believe he was an Inspector, he was always very civil), a fat nurse, (Wilson, I think) sat in a chair near her. I went in and I wished to kiss her, but the nurse interposed. I took no notice of her, and I kissed my child. I said in French to her, 'What are these people doing here?' The nurse said 'You must speak in English.' The Inspector said, 'I warn you madam, I shall write down what you say,' and he had paper and pencil. I said, 'You may write as much as you like, my friend, I have nothing to say, but it strikes me as very strange to see you in this room.' Mrs. Maybrick spoke up, 'Do, mammy dear, don't excite yourself, the Inspector is only doing his duty.' 'But,' I said, 'What is the nurse for, and the people outside? I consider it infamous, and Edwin seems to have lost his head. What on earth does it all mean?' Mrs Maybrick replied, 'They think I have poisoned Jim,' 'Poisoned Jim!' I said, 'Why if he is poisoned, he has poisoned himself – he made a perfect apothecaries' shop of himself, as we all know.' I then sat down near her and asked her a few questions, and she said in reply, 'Dr. Hopper and Mrs. Briggs and Michael believe me guilty, but mammy I am innocent.' I then went downstairs as the fat nurse suggested I should do. A thin nurse (Gore) was standing outside the door. I again got hold of Edwin, but I could obtain no further details than that an intrigue with a man had been discovered, and that they wanted an excuse to send Florie home to me, and keep the children, and to clinch matters they called in Dr. Carter and mentioned their suspicions, and that she had put something in the medicine. The first thing next morning, having had no detailed account of anything, I again saw Edwin, who told me, 'Florie swooned on Saturday on the sofa in the room where Jim was dying, and I took her up unconscious, and placed her on the bed in the spare room. She was completely unconscious until Monday. She never moved or spoke, and on Monday they had asked, so Mrs. Briggs told me, if I should be sent for, and she said 'No', - in fact, he said, 'They all lost their heads.'

Only with the benefit of this first-hand account it is possible to understand Edwin's state of mind at the time. He had been left behind to face the music, and unlike his cold and calculating older brother, was in a blind panic. He had simply joined forces with those wishing to see Florence back with her mother in Paris, under the cloud of having neglected James during his illness. Now James was dead, seemingly murdered by his sister-in-law, but following some very odd behaviour by Michael, with Edwin very much involved. No one was vaguely aware of the serial killer in their midst, using misguided envy within the household to further the aim of eliminating not only James, but Florence, the two people representing the real danger of suggesting, even light-heartedly, that Michael Maybrick was Jack the Ripper.

At ten o'clock I saw Alice Yapp. I asked who she was. The nurse in attendance said she was the children's nurse. I went to the nursery, and said to her, 'Are you Bobo and Gladys's nurse?' She replied, 'Yes.' 'How are the children?' She replied, 'Very well.' 'Are you the nurse that has been here so long?' She replied, 'Yes' 'And are you the one that has caused additional trouble to that poor young thing by showing letters you find?' She replied, 'She weren't a poor young thing then.' 'Well' I said, 'You are an ungrateful, disloyal servant.' Up to this time no-one had told me a word of what was in any letter.

After leaving Alice Yapp, I went to see Mrs. Maybrick, and said that if she would give me the name and street of her solicitor, I would go to Liverpool. I had never been about in Liverpool, and did not know the name of a street or my way. In fact, I was a complete stranger in Liverpool. I then saw Elizabeth Humphreys, the cook, for the first time. She said to me, 'I wish I could help missus – Baroness.' I replied, 'I wish you could, but I myself know nothing.' Before I started for Liverpool, I went in to Mrs. Maybrick, and said, 'I have been trying to get something out of Edwin, but I understand nothing. Will you tell me, my dear, what this talk of fly-papers meant, for Edwin has just said there were some fly-papers found. What were they for?' Mrs. Maybrick replied, 'Why, for cosmetics.' I then said to her in French, 'Tell me, have you really done anything wrong, my dear, to your husband?' She replied, 'No, mama, I swear to you I am innocent. I did put a powder he asked for in the meat juice, but he would not have it.' Here the nurse interposed – the thin one (Gore) and, in despair, I said, 'Well, I will go to Liverpool and return as soon as possible.'

The plan to simply oust Florence had back-fired, and all involved in the charade, organised by Michael, had not only lost their heads, but were fearful of being implicated. Michael had very wisely decided to distance himself from the scene, a course of action at which he was particularly adept, returning to London where it was his intention to seek out witnesses to Florence's weekend dalliance at Flatman's Hotel, a mission heartily endorsed by his fraternal ally, Superintendent Isaac Bryning, who, for his part, was busy in Liverpool organising the next phase of Florence's downfall.

No sooner had the Baroness arrived at the office of Richard and Arnold Cleaver, solicitors, on Saturday, 18th May, than a telegram was handed to Richard, 'If you wish to see her before she is removed, you had better hurry,' which they did, arriving at Battlecrease House to be met at the gate by local magistrate Colonel Bidwell, accompanied by clerk to the court, William Swift, together with Dr. Humphreys, Dr. Hopper, and Superintendent Bryning, who explained there was sufficient evidence to justify a remand in custody. At this point the Cleaver brothers, as Florence's lawyers, had a prime opportunity to demand evidence to justify such a course of action, but did nothing, giving rise for conjecture as to whether, after their fraternal discussion with Michael Maybrick and the police officers, Florence's lawyers were actually convinced of their client's innocence.

The Baroness was led courteously into a bedroom, whilst the main group, accompanied by a representative from the local press, made their way to Florence's bedroom, where Superintendent Bryning stood at the foot of the bed, and addressed the gathering.

> *Supt. Bryning:This person is Mrs. Maybrick, wife of the late James Maybrick. She is charged with having caused his death by administering poison to him. I understand her consent is*

	given to a remand, and therefore I need not introduce, nor give evidence.
William Swift:	You asked for a remand of eight days?
Supt. Bryning:	Yes, that is so.
Arnold Cleaver:	I appear for the prisoner. I consent to a remand.
Col. Bidwell:	Very well. That is all.

The Baroness had not only been refused access to Florence, but found herself locked in the bedroom, whilst Florence, unable to walk unaided, and hastily clad in the Baroness's hat and cloak, was carried out of the house in a chair and placed in a waiting cab, which slowly made its way to her new place of residence, Walton Gaol, on the outskirts of Liverpool. The Baroness was then released by a very embarrassed police constable. No evidence had been produced against Florence, nor indeed was there any, only 'particulars' provided by Bro. Michael Maybrick to Bro. Isaac Bryning, together with a collection of suspect bottles and packages collected from about the house by Michael Maybrick's acolytes. Bro. Richard Cleaver had ample grounds for objecting to the remand, but did nothing. Florence recalls her arrival at the prison gates.

After a two hour drive, we arrived at Walton Gaol, in the suburbs of Liverpool. I shuddered as I looked at the tall, gloomy building. A bell was ringing, and the big iron gates swung back, and allowed us to pass in. I was received by the governor, and immediately led away by a female warder. We crossed a small courtyard, and stopped at a door, which was unlocked and relocked. Then we passed down a narrow passage, to a door that led into a dark gloomy room. A bench ran along each side, a bare wooden table stood in the middle, and a weighing machine by the door. A female warder asked me to give up any valuables in my possession. These consisted of a watch, two diamond rings, and a brooch. Then I was asked to stand upon the weighing machine, and my weight was duly noted. These formalities completed, I was led through a building into a cell especially set apart for sick prisoners. I gazed around. At the bedside was a chair with a china cup containing milk, and a plate of bread upon it. The cell was bare. The light struggled in dimly through a dirty, barred window. The stillness was appalling, and I felt benumbed, a sense of terrible oppression weighted me down. If only someone would tell me whose diabolical mind had conceived and directed suspicion against me!.

Mrs. Maybrick's Story. Florence Maybrick.

THE BRIERLEY LETTER

Once the dust had settled on that fateful weekend at Flatman's Hotel, Florence had begun to engage in correspondence with Alfred Brierley, in the forlorn hope that the spark of romance could be re-ignited. At the same time, Superintendent Bryning was busy gathering evidence of Florence's adultery, with one particular item, the 'Brierley Letter', proving crucial in the prosecution case as substantiation of Florence's infidelity, and continued infatuation with her paramour.

There are two versions of the discovery of this letter. The first is the truth, the whole truth, and nothing but the truth. The other is the result of one man's phenomenal ability to create a skilfully contrived fabrication, sustaining credibility for over 130 years. The letter makes startling reading. Florence was clearly as besotted with Alfred Brierley as she was disenchanted with James, an unfortunate situation which would weigh heavily on Florence in the weeks to come.

Dearest,
Wednesday.

Your letter under cover to John K came to hand just after I had written to you on Monday. I did not expect to hear from you so soon, and delayed in giving him the necessary instructions. Since my return I have been nursing M all day and night. He is sick unto death. The doctors held a consultation yesterday, and now all depends how long his strength will hold out. Both my brothers-in-law are here, and we are terribly anxious. I cannot answer your letter fully today, my darling, but relieve your mind of all fear of discovery now and for the future. M has been delirious since Sunday, and I know that he is perfectly ignorant of everything, even as to the name of the street, and also that he has been making any inquiries whatsoever. The tale he told me was pure fabrication, and only intended to frighten the truth out of me.

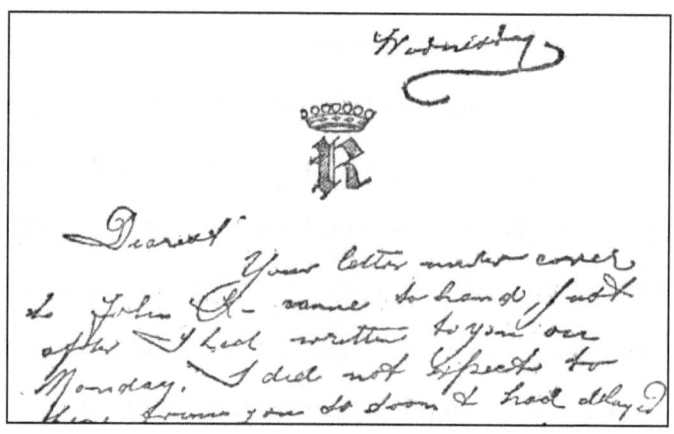

In fact, he believes my statement, although he will not admit it. You need not, therefore, go abroad on his account, dearest, but in any case please don't leave England until I have seen you once again. You must feel that those two letters of mine were written under circumstances which must ever excuse their injustice in your eyes. Do you suppose I should act as I am doing if I really felt and meant that I inferred them? If you wish to write to me about anything, do so now, as all the letters pass through my hands at present. Excuse this scrawl, my own darling, but I dare not leave the room for a moment, and I do not know when I shall be able to write to you again. In haste. Yours ever, Florie.

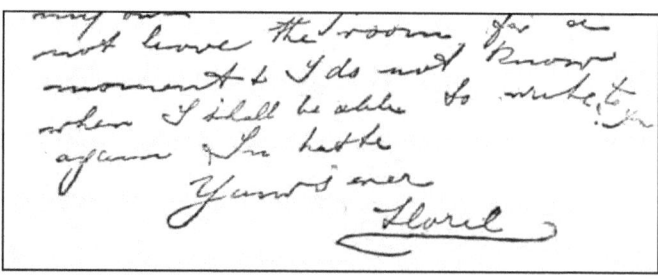

James had died on the evening of Saturday 11th May, and, after a very eventful week, Michael departed for London on Friday, 17th May, coincidentally encountering en route Florence's mother, Baroness von Roques. On arrival at Battlecrease House, the Baroness confronted Edwin, demanding an explanation of events, in the course of which he explained Alice Yapp's discovery of the Brierley letter as it fell from Florence's dress, during her swoon on Saturday, three days after Michael's arrival. Alice Yapp just couldn't resist opening the envelope and reading the letter, before passing it on to Edwin and relaying the contents to her friend, Alice Grant, the gardener's wife, who in turn passed on the tale to the kitchen servants, only four days after having gossiped with them about the fly-papers.

I have questioned Elizabeth Humphreys the cook, and Mary Cadwallader the parlour-maid, as to when they first heard about this letter, and they tell me on the night of the 11th May, after James Maybrick's death, Alice Grant, the gardener's wife, came into the kitchen and told them that a love-letter of Mrs. Maybrick's had been picked up.

Alexander MacDougall.

The servants took no further notice of the matter, and, at the time, Michael Maybrick would have been totally unaware of this discovery. However, once handed the letter by Edwin, probably the following day, he realised that not only was the document explosively incriminating against Florence, but it could potentially be used for his own personal betterment. Over the next few days, he mulled over how to make the most of the situation. James was now dead, Florence was languishing in Walton Goal, and before long questions were bound to be asked in a court of law. Michael soon came to realise that his unjustified remonstrations of suspicion may have been interpreted as an over-reaction to the fly-paper fantasies of a children's nurse, and hardly sufficient excuse for his over-zealous behaviour. If, however, the Brierley letter were to have been found and presented on the day of his arrival at Battlecrease House, this would provide valid grounds for suspecting Florence's involvement in her husband's imminent death, and ample justification for approaching the doctors at the first possible opportunity. However, Alice Yapp's co-operation, allegiance even, would be crucial, if such a scheme were to succeed.

On the day after his arrival, Michael had listened intently as Alice recounted the discovery of the flypapers, suggesting an affinity with the Higgins trial, which had ended on the scaffold at Walton prison. This was, of course, not their first meeting, as Alice had been employed at Battlecrease House for over five years, but the couple had never really spoken at length before. Now, the more Michael engaged Alice in conversation, the more he had come to realise that he actually related to this like minded young lady from the respectable family in Shropshire, well educated, intelligent, and above all possessed of a fiery resilience. Had he inadvertently stumbled upon the personification of a woman with whom he could interact, in an otherwise misogynistic existence?

Before long it became apparent that they both disliked Florence Maybrick with a vengeance. Alice, for her part, had been both flattered and delighted to discourse freely with the famous celebrity, who seemed to regard her as an equal, an art at which he had become particularly well versed on the streets of Whitechapel. Edwin was certainly an attractive man with whom she had soon developed a rapport on his return from America, hopefully unnoticed by the other servants, but Michael exuded a presence, a haughty charisma, a man who clearly commanded the respect of others, yet with such a disarming smile, and such deep penetrating eyes. In Alice's eyes, their age difference was less than that between James and Florence, and this meeting could prove to be a life changing event. Alice was under his spell, and Michael knew it. It had worked so many times before.

When Michael explained his plan, Alice, relieved of possible repercussions for having opened and read the letter when it fell from Florence's dress, mentioned an occurrence from the previous week. Florence had entrusted a letter to Alice for delivery at the post-office, en-route to which baby Gladys had accidentally dropped the letter in the gutter, causing mud to stain the address, giving Alice an excuse to open the envelope. That particular letter contained nothing of interest, but Alice was quite capable of re-living the event as if it were on the Wednesday of Michael's arrival in Liverpool, providing justification for her opening the Brierley letter. If that was what Michael wanted? Edwin had not been too enthusiastic over the idea, but would, of course, do as Michael said, agreeing to confirm receipt of the letter from Alice on the Wednesday evening.

Alice's story, under the contrivance of master puppeteer Michael Maybrick, would benefit further if the date could be substantiated, so why not just add the word 'Wednesday' to the top of the letter, a seemingly simple solution, and with three 'witnesses' to the handover on the Wednesday, credibility would be assured. Solid grounds for Michael's unduly suspicious behaviour from the moment of arrival, and proof of the extent to which forward planning had always been crucial to the man's apparent invincibility.

On examination of the letter, however, the word 'Wednesday' appears suspect, displaying marked inconsistencies with Florence's usual handwriting. Compare for instance, the 'day' in 'Wednesday' with the 'day' in 'Monday' on the fourth line of the same letter. Compare the very laboured flourish beneath the 'Wednesday' and that beneath Florence's signature in the same letter, and in another letter written by Florence whilst in Walton Prison. Also note in this latter letter, the very different 'W' in 'Walton' compared to the 'Wednesday' in the Brierley letter. How unfortunate also, that the perpetrator of the amendment had overlooked the content of the letter, which refers to the

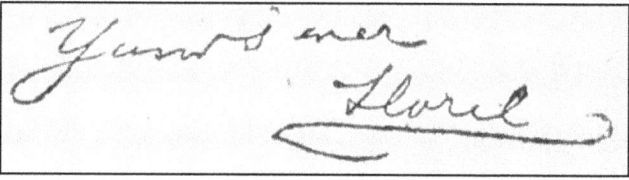

Brierley Letter. Genuine signature

Walton Gaol Letter. Genuine signature

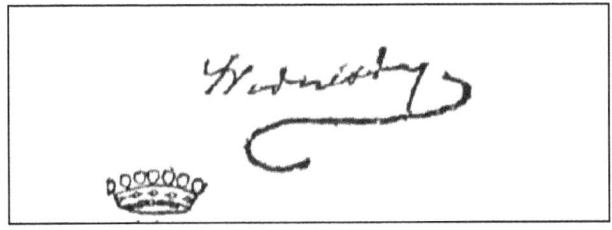

Suspect 'Wednesday', Brierley Letter

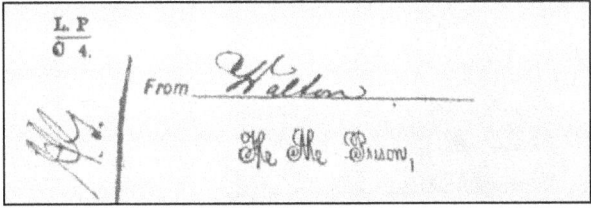

Walton Gaol Letter. Florence's Handwriting.

presence of both brothers-in-law at Battlecrease House during Wednesday, although Michael did not arrive until later in the evening, after the letter had purportedly been handed over. The letter must have been written after his arrival. A crucial oversight. Furthermore, let there be no doubt that if Michael Maybrick had been in possession of the Brierley letter on the Wednesday, the day of his arrival, he would have been flourishing it under the nose of Dr. Humphreys, whom he called upon later that night, and Dr. Carter, on their first encounter the following evening.

So the word 'Wednesday' was added, and the fabrication involving the handover of the letter rehearsed again and again, until the time was ripe for it to be revealed in spectacular fashion, and accepted as fact for the next 130 years.

INQUEST

THE SCENE AT THE CORONER'S INQUEST ON THE DEATH OF THE LATE MR. MAYBRICK

The adjourned inquest was opened at the Wellington Reading Rooms, Garston, on the 28th May, attracting an attendance of some five hundred people and a large crowd outside, awaiting Florence's arrival from Walton Gaol. The Crown was represented by barrister Douglas Steel, the next door neighbour conveniently summoned by Michael Maybrick to witness the surprise discovery of the arsenic stache found by Alice Yapp. Such a small world. Also representing the Crown were Bros. Isaac Bryning and Richard Baxendale. To represent Florence Maybrick, Bro. Richard Cleaver had appointed barrister Bro. William Pickford, of Apollo University Lodge No.357, of which the Lord Chamberlain, the Earl of Lathom, was a fellow member. Five years earlier, William Pickford had defended the two women charged with murder in the Flanagan case, in which arsenic from flypapers had been used to poison the victim. Possibly not the most apt choice of barrister, as both lives had ended in a sensational double hanging at Walton Gaol, the very place where Florence was now incarcerated, a fact which had not escaped the forty journalists present, always on alert for the next newsworthy headline. Florence had not fully recovered from her mysterious swoon, compounded by the stress of being inexplicably imprisoned in Walton Gaol, and speculation was rife as to Florence's state of mind, especially when the news was belatedly announced that the prisoner would not be appearing at the inquest that day.

What has become known to the locals as the Aigburth Mystery reached a more crucial stage yesterday, when the police unfolded the first part of their budget of evidence before Mr .Coroner Brighouse. It had been arranged that the largest public room of which Garston can boast should be placed at the disposal of the authorities, and the old police court in Wellington Road was accordingly hired for the purpose. It was certainly roomy enough to accommodate the elaborate array of lawyers, reporters, witnesses and spectators who attended, but from an acoustic point of view it was about as bad a building as could have been selected. The press-men experienced the utmost difficulty in hearing, and for the twelve mortal hours over which the proceedings extended, many of them had to take note in all positions, standing up between serried ranks of policemen, on their knees, sometimes almost on the backs of learned counsel, and in various other awkward postures, for it was found impossible to hear at the tables assigned to them. The intense and very widespread interest taken in this remarkable poisoning case was sufficiently evident by the presence of members of the press from distant parts of the country, and it was noticed that among the spectators were some eminent toxicologists.

The Coroner, as if to make amends for the secrecy with which he carried out the preliminary inquest, was extremely courteous to the thirty or forty journalists who were drawn to the spot, and it is only fair to say that he made the best arrangements in his power to provide for their comfort. In the gallery, far out of earshot, were congregated a knot of persons who might be said to represent the British public, and who doubtless imagined that, if they could not hear what was going on, they would at least enjoy the luxury of a good stare at the unhappy lady, the leading actress in this moving drama. But in such an expectation they were doomed to disappointment, inasmuch as Mrs. Maybrick was not in a fit condition to make her appearance, though the Coroner intimated that it will be necessary for her to do so before the inquest terminated. Therefore there will be opportunity for the gratification of curiosity when she eventually appears.

Liverpool Daily Post. 28 May 1889.

The purpose of an inquest is to determine cause of death. There is no accused person, and evidence is admitted at the discretion of the Coroner, such evidence to be relative to ascertaining the cause of death. The inquest of the 14th May had been adjourned, pending analysis of body parts removed at the post mortem, and the Crown's case relied on the assumption that arsenic would be found. Imagine then the reaction of the Coroner and police officers when, just prior to resumption of the proceedings, the analyst, Mr. Edward Davies, informed them that no significant evidence of arsenic had been found in the body parts. The police were now in a

> **THE MAYBRICK CASE**
> ———
> **A NEW THEORY—ALLEGED MADNESS OF MRS MAYBRICK**

very compromising situation of their own making, with Florence languishing in prison on suspicion of murder, and the newspaper reporters brandishing their sharpened pencils only yards away.

At an unbiased hearing, the results of the analysis would have been disclosed to the Court, and the Crown prosecution case would have evaporated, followed by Florence's release from police custody, but Coroner Brighouse and Superintendent Bryning were having none of that, deciding to withhold the results of the post mortem findings, and issue an order for the exhumation of James Maybrick's body for further analysis. No explanation was provided at the hearing as to why the results of the post-mortem analysis had not been announced, or why exhumation and further analysis were considered necessary. What had led Coroner Brighouse and the police to believe that different results would be obtained by taking further body samples? Had a compliant expert already been selected for the task? The local newspapers soon picked up on this unusual situation,

The case against Mrs. Maybrick is a weak one, with the exhumation indicating a need to root up in all directions points which might tell against her.
Liverpool Mercury. 1 June 1889.

The exhumation of the late Mr. Maybrick's body, and the circumstance under which it took place, were alike extraordinary. The disentombing of remains, which have, prior to internment, been subjected to a post-mortem examination, is unusual, and it was believed that the Coroner had considered this step necessary because the result of the analysis of the viscera had not been such as expected.
Liverpool Courier. 1 June 1889.

Michael Maybrick's persuasive insistence on Florence's guilt had already convinced Coroner Brighouse and Superintendent Bryning, who were now intent on creating a second opportunity to eke out evidence of arsenic in the body of a man prone to self-dosing with poisonous substances. Coroner Brighouse opened proceedings by addressing the jury,

Gentlemen, you are summoned here to investigate the circumstances attending the death of the late James Maybrick, the inquest on whose body was formally opened on the 14th of this month. Since that time the wife of the deceased has been apprehended by the police, charged with having caused the death of her late husband, and it will be for you to say, after hearing all the evidence, whether you consider she is criminally responsible for the death of her husband. The Inquiry will eventually be adjourned for a week, in order that the analysis of the deceased's viscera by Mr. Davies may be completed. Mrs. Maybrick is not here today, but sooner or later she will have to be present in order that she may be identified by a witness.

Coroner Brighouse

The first witness to be called was Michael Maybrick, who immediately proceeded to accuse Florence of negligence in not having summoned a professional nurse and second doctor earlier. Mr. Pickford then began to address a few pertinent questions, relating to the strange sequence of events concerning the Lady Superintendent, and inferring that perhaps Michael Maybrick may have been more involved than he was prepared to admit.

On Friday 10th May, did you see Nurse Gore?' 'I did, about 11 o'clock.' 'Was she coming off duty at the time?' 'She was.' 'About one o'clock the same day, had you been to Liverpool?' 'No.' 'Between eleven and one o'clock the same day, had Nurse Gore been out of the house?' 'Yes.' 'Do you *happen to know where she had been?' ' I think to see the matron, but I do not know.' 'In consequence of what she told you, did you go anywhere?' 'I did, into my brother's bedroom' 'And what did you do?' 'I took possession of a little bottle of Valentine's Meat Juice.' 'When you gave the meat extract to Dr. Carter, was it in the same condition in which you had taken possession of it?' 'It was in the same condition.'*

William Pickford was obtusely inferring connivance with the bottle of meat juice, but to no avail. Michael Maybrick had denied going to Liverpool, where the Nursing Institution was located, and had denied tampering with the Valentine's Meat Juice. Mr. Pickford had his suspicions, the imperturbable Michael Maybrick knew it, but nobody else present had the faintest idea of the motive behind this line of questioning. The Lady Superintendent was never called upon to give evidence, a crucial omission which would have radically altered matters, had William Pickford rightly pursued this mysterious sequence of events.

By now the Aigburth Mystery had developed into something of a soap opera in the local press, and whilst those fortunate enough clamoured to attend the live performance in the Wellington Rooms, most relied on the skill of the journalists in the courtroom to bring the actors to life in their daily columns.

Amongst those who personally caused a little thrill of sensation was Mr. A. Brierley, whose name figures so notoriously in a certain peculiar phrase of the exposé. This gentleman, who cannot by the wildest stretch of the feminine imagination be likened to an Adonis, seated himself at a corner of the reporters' table. He was the cynosure of all eyes who knew him, but his cool and unconcerned air apparently indicated that he did not take as grave a view of the part which he plays in these revelations as other people would be disposed to do. Another gentleman who attracted interest of quite a different order was Mr. Michael Maybrick, the well-known musical composer, who has written delightful well known English ballads under the nom de plume of 'Stephen Adams'. As one of the principal witnesses for the prosecution, as the brother of the deceased gentleman, and in his capacity as an eminent man in the musical world, he was throughout a good portion of the proceedings, literally 'en evidence.'

Liverpool Daily Post. 28 May 1889.

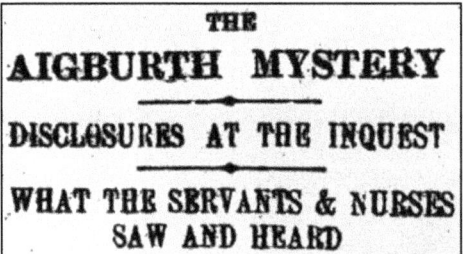

Alice Yapp, seated next to Michael Maybrick, had been watching the proceedings for three hours, and the seriousness of the situation was slowly dawning. Alice's involvement in this possible murder scenario had been entirely of her own making, the result of a brooding resentment and irresistible urge for revenge, regarded as attributes by her mentor Michael Maybrick, whose confidence and composure in giving evidence had provided some measure of reassurance for the task ahead. As ready as she would ever be, on hearing her name called, Alice Yapp walked up to the stand, carefully recounting the story she had been rehearsing for the last three weeks.

The next witness called was Alice Yapp, an intelligent woman apparently about the same age as Mrs. Maybrick, and who was the nurse at Battlecrease House. From the beginning it was obvious that her evidence was regarded by Superintendent Bryning as of great importance.

Liverpool Daily Post. 29 May 1889.

This was the occasion on which details of the Brierley letter would be revealed for the first time, having hitherto been privy to three people only. Prior to disclosure at this inquest, nobody else in Battlecrease House had the slightest clue of the existence of this closely guarded document.

'I heard of the dropped letter and its contents for the first time at the Coroner's Court.' Dr. Edward Carter. Liverpool Chirurgical Journal 1890.

'When did you first hear anything about the letter opened by Alice Yapp?' 'I knew nothing about it until it was publicly mentioned.'

Matilda Briggs. Liverpool Daily Post. 15 August 1889.

'I have questioned Elizabeth Humphreys, the cook, and Mary Cadwallader the parlour maid, as to when they first heard about this letter, and they tell me they did not hear anything about what was in the letter until it was read at the Coroner's inquest.'

Alexander MacDougall.

Alice performed well, explaining how baby Gladys had dropped Florence's letter in the mud en route to the post office on the Wednesday of Michaels arrival. Everyone believed the story.

No such interest has been observed in a Coroner's Court for a long time as that which was shown in the statement of the children's nurse, Alice Yapp. Interest in her story grew as she told it, and when she described how Mrs. Maybrick's letter fell into the mud on its conveyance to the post office, and how, in getting a fresh envelope to re-address it, she caught a glimpse of the words 'My Darling', the court hung on every sentence, and the silence was complete. The Coroner read that extraordinary letter deliberately, and with emphasis, and when he had finished there was a movement of chairs, a rustling of dresses, and a clearing of throats as if a painful ordeal had been passed. The story of the flypapers did not eclipse the story told by these letters, but simply deepened and strengthened the impression produced.

Liverpool Daily Post. 28 May 1889.

Alice then responded to routine questions regarding the search of Battlecrease House for incriminating evidence, and eventually resumed her seat on the witness bench, rightly pleased with herself. Her mentor watched on, expressionless, but content. The subject of James Maybrick's will was then introduced into proceedings, and Michael Maybrick was recalled to give evidence.

Mr. Steel:	*Mr. Michael Maybrick would rather not have the will read unless it is material to the case.*
Coroner:	*This will was sealed, and you found it sealed?*
Maybrick:	*Yes.*
Coroner:	*Mrs. Maybrick would have no knowledge of its contents?*
Maybrick:	*No, I don't think she even knew about it.*
Coroner:	*I thought it was suggested that the will was very much in favour of the widow, and that she had an opportunity of knowing it.*

No such evidence favouring the widow had been presented to the Court, and Coroner Brighouse had no justification whatsoever for making such an inference. Michael Maybrick, however, had every reason not to reveal the contents of the will, which would have positively ruled out financial gain as a motive for murder, and despite Mr. Pickford's arguments to the contrary, Coroner Brighouse seemed only too pleased to oblige, ruling without further ado that the contents of the will be withheld from the Court.

After all the evidence had been heard, and before close of proceedings, the matter was raised of John Dalglish's discharge as jury foreman at the previous hearing. William Pickford, representing Florence Maybrick, now had the opportunity of opening a powerful defence strategy by exposing James Maybrick's drug addiction, endorsed by John Dalglish's impending evidence.

Mr. Pickford: *I understand a communication was made to you, Mr. Coroner, on the first meeting, 14th May, by a gentleman originally sworn in as foreman of the jury, and I should like to know whether it is proposed to call him or not?*

Coroner: *No.*

Mr. Pickford: *I understand it was something important that that the gentleman thought that he might not sit upon the jury?*

Coroner: *I feel certain it is not relevant. The foreman went to see the body and then made a statement. I communicated it to Mr. Steel, who was then acting for the relatives, and to Superintendent Bryning, and I said, If you think the*

> *statement is useful to you, and that it is evidence, and that the foreman ought to appear as a witness, then I will discharge him. They both thought it would be the better course for me to discharge him, and I did so.*

Mr. Steel was barrister for the Crown, and the relatives were Crown witnesses Michael and Edwin Maybrick. Hardly surprising that they and Superintendent Bryning, aware of the damning nature of the intended disclosure, had no wish to reveal to the court the former juryman's evidence. William Pickford, however, representing Florence, and with no inclination whatsoever to discharge the witness, had received no prior contact from the Coroner.

Mr. Pickford: I rather gathered it had been a statement favourable to my client Mrs. Maybrick , or contrary to the theory set up against her, and I supposed the gentleman had been warned to be present. Do you say it was a matter you would not allow to go before the jury?

Coroner: I ought not to tell the jury. The gentleman called upon Mr. Cleaver and gave him his statement, and therefore it rests with Mr. Cleaver or Mr. Bryning to call him.

Mr. Pickford: That is not quite correct.

Indeed it is not. Regardless of the communication having been originally made to Mr. Cleaver, it had been addressed at the previous hearing directly to the Coroner, who at the time found the statement sufficiently important to agree to the foreman's retirement, with a view to appearing as a witness at this re-convened inquest. The decision to call Mr. Dalglish rested with the Coroner, who had no good reason to refuse, but was nonetheless resolute in his determination not to allow the statement. What, other than Michael Maybrick's influence, had caused Coroner Brighouse to change his mind in the intervening period?

Coroner: *It was a statement made by the deceased, and not in the presence of a certain other person. The deceased was not at the time in fear of death, and I don't see how the statement could be evidence.*

Mr. Pickford: *I understand it was a statement as to the cause of his illness made to this gentleman. It certainly would not be evidence against my client, but whether it would be evidence as to the cause of death, I don't know. I confess I have not the knowledge you have as to what is evidence at investigations of this kind, if hostile it would not be evidence against my client.*

Coroner: *I think you have gathered when Mr. Bryning has given evidence which would not be evidence before the Magistrates, I have ruled against it. At the same time, I feel I have a roving commitment to take evidence as tendered, presuming it may apply to A, B, C, or D.*

Mr. Pickford: *I say no more about it, if you don't think it right to go before the jury. Whether it would be evidence as to cause of death, I don't know. I confess I have not the*

> *knowledge you have as to what is evidence at investigations of this kind.*

Samuel Brighouse had been a Coroner for four years, whilst William Pickford just happened to be an experienced barrister of fifteen years standing, and President of the Law Society, yet here he was, confessing to having less knowledge than the Coroner, conceding a perfectly viable argument, and letting the matter drop. So much for Florence Maybrick's defence team. Not only was Coroner Brighouse resolute that John Dalglish's statement should remain off the record, but Florence's lawyers were prepared to meekly acquiesce in this blatant disregard of evidence in their client's favour.

By the close of proceedings at 9.00 p.m., absolutely no evidence had been heard relating to cause of death, the very purpose for which the Court had been convened. The question has to be asked, would Coroner Brighouse, Bro. Superintendent Isaac Bryning, and indeed Bro. William Pickford, have conducted proceedings in such an extraordinary manner, were it not for the desire to appease Bro. Michael Maybrick? The inquest was adjourned, yet again, until the 5th June.

A word of praise is due to Superintendent Bryning, not only for the succinct and indefatigable way in which he laid his evidence before the jury, but for the skilful manner in which he examined and re-examined the various witnesses who he called. He was quite equal to the occasion, and the best proof of his ability consisted in the fact that he left not the slightest loophole for the learned counsel arranged against him

Liverpool. Daily Post. 28 May 1889.

TRIAL BY NEWSPAPER

Within hours of the doors closing on the Wellington Rooms, a grim cortege made its way through the gates of Anfield Cemetery.

The night was perfectly black and the stillness of the cemetery appalling. Across the gravel path that runs past the grave there had been placed two benches obtained from the adjacent catacombs. Here the party, who had been silent and pre-occupied, stopped and the grave-diggers lighted their naphtha lamps, the light from which cast a faint and sickly glow over the surrounding tombstones. However, the men got quickly to work, ropes were fastened to the handles of the coffin, and in a moment it was raised, its mounting yet untarnished with rust. It was placed with its end upon the two benches, then commenced the operation of unscrewing the lid. This, of course, did not take long, but there was scarcely anyone present who did not feel an involuntary shudder as the pale worn features of the dead appeared in the flickering rays of a lamp held over the coffin. The body was not removed from its receptacle. What everyone remarked was that, although interred a fortnight, the corpse was wonderfully preserved. There were scarcely any signs of corruption, the only thing noticeable was that whilst the extremities, the feet and the lower part of the legs and hands remained their natural colour, the rest of the body had turned a dark blue. As the dissecting knife of Dr. Barron pursued its rapid and skilful work there was, however, whenever a slight breath of wind blew, an odour of corruption. The doctor removed in succession his lungs, heart, kidneys, and part of the thigh bone; coming to the head he cut out the tongue, and opening the skull removed one half of the brain. Each part as it was removed was place in a large stone jar, which was covered over securely with a canvas cloth, and then sealed with Dr. Barron's seal. This done, the remains were then re-

covered, the coffin silently and expediently lowered again into the vault, and the benches were replaced in the catacombs. The jar was taken into one of the vehicles, which about midnight moved slowly and in silence towards the entrance of the cemetery. The others who had been engaged in the horrible business left immediately afterwards, glad that it was all over.
Liverpool Daily Post. 1 June 1889.

Every available copy of the newspaper was snapped up by the general public, savouring the perverse thrill of the exhumation, and eagerly awaiting reports on the ensuing inquest. Newspaper sales trebled, as the Aigburth Mystery became the talk of the town.

The Aigburth poisoning mystery was advanced another stage yesterday, when Mrs. Maybrick for the second time appeared in semi-private before a magistrate at Walton Gaol, and was once again remanded on the charge of killing her husband by the administration of poisoning. The mystery surrounding Mr. Maybrick's death seems to deepen, and to have taken a greater hold upon the public mind. Mrs. Maybrick's condition is still the subject of much speculation. On the one hand she is reported to be quite well, and on the other that the state of her health does not permit her being removed from the gaol. These conflicting statements have excited great surprise, and been not a little commented upon. The most diverse theories are put forward to account for her 'mysterious illness', but it would be manifestly unfair to give expression to the wild rumours that are afloat. Yesterday, Mrs. Maybrick was visited by her mother, the Baroness Roques, who, it is said, has been proffered assistance and advice in connection with the charges by her American friends. The distressed lady is taking very active steps for the defence of her daughter, of whose innocence she seems profoundly sure. One of the rumours prevalent on the Exchange is to the effect that an important line of defence will be the theory that Mr. Maybrick's death was the result of poisoning by strychnine, an overdose of which, it is alleged, he had inadvertently taken. Whether this is true or not, it would be difficult to say, but in the present excited state of public opinion, any conjecture of the kind is eagerly received and discussed.

Liverpool Courier. 1 June 1889.

The most startling rumour that has yet been heard about the Aigburth poisoning mystery was that which our representative had yesterday from a very reliable source. From this report it would seem to be a question not as to how the late Mr. James Maybrick was poisoned, but as to whether he died at all from poisoning. Our informant, who is credited with being in possession of official information, states that the quantity of poison found in the intestines has been found to be so small as not to amount to anything serious, or which could possibly destroy human life. If there be good foundation for this astounding revelation, then the chances are that the case against Mrs. Maybrick may collapse, for under such circumstances it is scarcely probable that the police would be able to sustain the charge of murder by the administration of poison.

THE AIGBURTH MYSTERY.

ALLEGED REMARKABLE DISCOVERY.

POSSIBLE COLLAPSE OF THE CASE.

Liverpool Daily Post. 3 June 1889.

One week later, on the 5th June, the inquest was once again re-convened. Florence was conveyed by carriage to the Wellington Reading Rooms, where she was accommodated in an ante-room, observed by a reporter from the Liverpool Weekly News.

Mrs. Maybrick was neatly attired in a Russian morning cloak, with bands of crepe running down the front. A coquettish net veil just reached the tip of her nose, while the long widow's veil hung gracefully behind. Beneath this, covering the best part of her brow, was a carefully curled fringe, which considerably enhanced her personal charms. Her hair was also worn at the back in the shape of a fringe, and altogether she presented a by no means unattractive appearance. Her figure is petite, and seen in the full light her complexion is much fairer than when observed in the gloomy precincts of Walton Prison.

THE AIGBURTH MYSTERY

THE INQUEST

ASTOUNDING EVIDENCE

SENSATIONAL DISCLOSURES

Liverpool Weekly News. 8 June 1889.

In the light of publicity, the shortcomings of Florence Maybrick's legal advisers had not gone unnoticed, and barrister William Pickford opened by immediately drawing the attention of the Coroner to the purpose of the inquest.

Mr. Pickford: *I think, before going any further in this case, we should have some evidence as to the cause death?*

Coroner: *It is a pity, Mr. Pickford, that this application was not made before.*

A sarcastic deflection of responsibility by Coroner Brighouse, who was primarily responsible for having allowed unrelated evidence to be heard before having established cause of death. This would continue as Coroner Brighouse chose to court the press, rather than announce the medical facts. The analyst, Edward Davies, was in the building, ready to declare the results of the latest tests as the basis for Florence's indictment or release, but in flagrant disregard of protocol, Superintendent Bryning was allowed by Coroner Brighouse to call the other witnesses first, leaving the way open for a slow and deliberate character assassination of Florence Maybrick, lapped up by the forty journalists present.

Under the guidance of the Superintendent, Dr. Hopper provided lengthy accounts of Florence's indebtedness, matrimonial difficulties, and physical confrontation with James after the Grand National, with evidence next provided by Dr. Carter and Dr. Humphreys, who, following Michael Maybrick's intervention, seemed intent on affirming suspicions of arsenic poisoning, despite previous reluctance to do so. Repeated reference to incriminating 'suggestions' played a crucial part in this scenario, yet neither doctor was prepared to name Michael Maybrick as the perpetrator, nor unaccountably, was William Pickford.

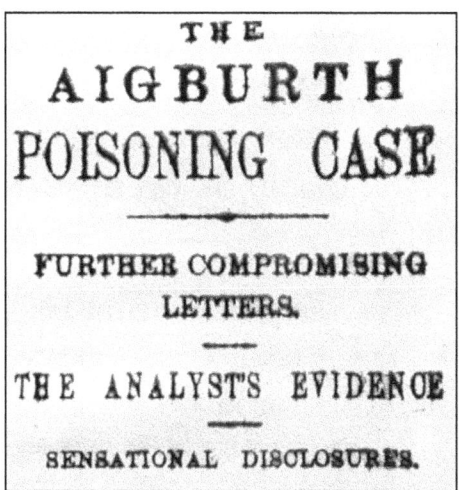

Attention was next directed towards Florence's conduct at Flatman's Hotel in March, which should have been irrelevant, prior to establishing evidence as to the cause of death. Nonetheless, Florence's character was about to be besmirched, with damning evidence provided by Flatman's Hotel waiter, Alfred Schweisso, sought out by Michael Maybrick whilst in London during the recess. Schweisso identified Florence, ushered briefly into court from the ante-room, and Albert Brierley, seated in the spectators gallery, as having spent the night together in the hotel, causing such a stir that Coroner Brighouse had to gavel for silence, under threat of having the room cleared. The press scribbled furiously. Society adultery sold newspapers.

The next day, evidence was provided by Edwin Maybrick, outlining routine events at Battlecrease House and at James's workplace, followed by another account of the discovery of various boxes and parcels. When the questioning moved to the subject of the Brierley letter, Edwin, never at ease in the witness box, and wondering just how he had become embroiled in this nightmare, showed signs of nervousness, first stating that Alice Yapp had handed over the letter in the road, then amending the location to the morning room. Nobody attached any significance to the hesitancy and uncertainty in his account.

Coroner Brighouse then announced the long awaited appearance of the analyst, with the test results. Journalists jostled for position, spectators coughed and shuffled their chairs, followed by silence as Mr. Edward Davies took his place on the stand. Described in the press as 'a business-like little man with grey hair, a slight beard, and spectacles,' the analyst embarked on a lengthy clinical evaluation of the processes involved in disseminating the chemical content of the various liquids, powders and body parts. Excitement and anticipation slowly evaporated into incomprehension and boredom, as Mr. Davies rambled on and on. Eventually, it was established that arsenic had been found in varying quantities in the powders and liquids found by Maybrick's privately convened search party, and, unsurprisingly, in the Valentine's Meat Juice which he had handed to Dr. Carter. Most importantly, however, only negligible traces of arsenic had been found in the body parts removed at the post mortem, or in the stomach and intestines removed at the exhumation, with a mere one fiftieth of a grain found in the liver. At last, the swell of evidence was moving in Florence's favour, leaving many bewildered at this change of fortune. Divisions were being formed in the minds of the general public, but Florence was now branded an adulteress, still in prison on a charge of suspected murder.

It was now time for the Coroner to address the jury, who, after thirty five minutes retirement, unhesitatingly returned a verdict of death by administration of irritant poison, administered by Florence Maybrick. Coroner Brighouse then asked for Florence to be brought into the courtroom,

Coroner: Florence Elizabeth Maybrick. The jury have inquired into the circumstances attending the death of your husband, and they have come to the conclusion that he has been wilfully murdered by you. I therefore commit you to the next Assizes to be held at Liverpool, there to take your trial upon that charge.

On the 8th June, James Maybrick's Death Certificate was issued, citing cause of death as 'Irritant poison administered to him by Florence Elizabeth Maybrick. Wilful murder'. Regardless of the outcome of a potentially impending trial, Florence Maybrick would appear on James Maybrick's Death

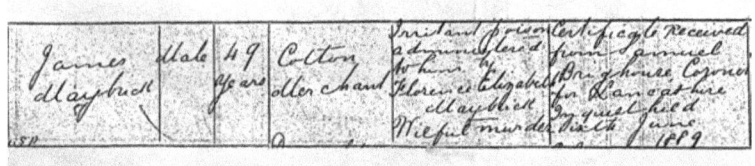

Certificate as the perpetrator. Two weeks earlier, on the morning of Saturday 25th May, removal vans had arrived outside Battlecrease House, under supervision of the Maybrick brothers, following which the contents of the house were removed and sold by auction, leaving Battlecrease House empty with Michael Maybrick as keyholder.

Despite imprisonment in Walton Gaol, press reports based solely on prosecution evidence, and the wording of the Death Certificate, Florence Maybrick was still innocent in the eyes of the law, with proceedings dependent on the outcome of the Magistrates Criminal Court, to be held on the 12th June in Islington, Liverpool. This was the first occasion on which Florence had appeared in court, and she listened attentively to proceedings, as the same witnesses recounted their evidence.

Alice Yapp took the stand to repeat her version of events, but was beginning to confuse her lies,

Coroner's inquest: *I went into the linen closet to put the children's clothes in.*

Magistrate's Court: *I went into the linen closet to get out a trunk, to get from it the children's clothing.*

SALE BY AUCTION.

THIS DAY, THE LATE JAMES MAYBRICK, Esq.,

by ORDER OF THE TRUSTEES

Handsome FURNITURE, elegant Ornaments, Continental Porcelain, Silver Plate, Electro Articles, Costly Jewels and Gold Watch, Paintings, and other Contents from the Residence 'Battlecrease', Grassendale,

REMOVED TO THE HANOVER ROOMS, MESSRS. BRANCH & LEETE

This day (Tuesday), 9th inst. At eleven o'clock, in the Hanover Rooms.

THE FASHIONABLE AND MODERN HOUSEHOLD FURNITURE. Cottage pianoforte by Collard and Collard in rosewood. Bronze groups, items of decoration expensive clocks, mantle side ornaments. Water colour drawings, a selection of oil paintings, and the important work,'The Village School', by Fabius. Small safe by Cartwright and Sons.

ELECTROPLATE AND SILVER WATCHES, JEWELS and PERSONAL ORNAMENTS of beauty and taste, comprising gold keyless watch with monogram, and open dial. Diamond and pearl brooches. Massive gold and bangle bracelet, set with Brazilian diamonds. Child's silver cup. Kettle drum. Tea,service of exquisite workmanship worked in gold. Heavy gold locket with interlaced initial letters. Case holding twelve large silver forks, antique pattern. Case of twelve teaspoons. Pair of sugar tongs. and caddy spoon, designed very beautifully. Six toddy spoons and sugar nippers of Oriental pattern. Pastry server. Nut crackers. Fruit spoons. Service of thread pattern of silver spoons and forks. Oval coffee tray. Four handsome dish covers. Cake baskets. Condiment frames. Japanese table gong. Set of twelve fish knives and forks. Salad Bowl. Candlesticks. Egg boiler. Oval breakfast dish with revolving cover. Crumb gatherer. Salters. Tea spoons with apostle handles. Biscuit barrel. Hammered tray for afternoon tea use. Sugar basket. Hot water jugs. Fruit spoons with decorated handles. Small tea services. Grecian formed silver claret ewer. Cayenne castors. Melon shaped teapot. Scrolled-chased tea service with bouquet vignettes. Salt cellars. Meat and poultry carvers. etc.

FEW CHOICE PAINTINGS AND DRAWINGS IN WATER COLOURS

A.HOBSON	A.PROCTOR	ARTHUR COX
MARY HAGGARTY	S.VEEVKKR	E.PAWIS
E.GOODALL R.A	N.SMITH	ALBERT HARTLAND
W.J.WADHAM	W.H.MURPHY	A.LEE ROGERS.
H.HILTON	C.E.BOULT	

OILS: 'Fair, Storm and Calm'; G.V,de Laar,'Quiet Corner'; F.R.Stock, 'Fruit'; James Poulton, 'Nature's Glow'; J.H.Hawthorne, 'Ancient Italy', 'Early Breakfast'; C.J.Lyden, 'Reconnoitring Party'; G.Nyon, 'Evening'; W.Davis, 'A.Fluke'; J.T.Steadman, 'Scotch Fishing Boat'; E.Ellis, 'Lledr Bridge'; H.A.Whittle, 'A.Nibble'; J.Fabius,'The Village School'. To be viewed prior to the hour of the sale, and catalogues can be had in the Hanover Galleries or at the offices of Messrs. Branch and Leete.

Neither version was the truth. Alice had been specifically instructed by Michael Maybrick to find Florence's trunk, and move it into a different room. Nobody noticed, and even Alice, lost in her lies, was probably unaware of her error. An interesting observation from the Magisterial hearing was picked up by lawyer J.H. Levy,

The examination of Mr. Maybrick before the Magistrates brought out a fact which may be worth noticing, viz, that sometime after his arrival at Battlecrease House, Mrs. Maybrick suggested that Dr. Fuller should be sent for to see her husband, but Michael replied that he was satisfied with Dr. Carter, who, he thought, understood the case at last.

J. H. Levy

Given the ongoing mystery surrounding the suspect London medicine, Dr. Fuller was the last person Michael Maybrick needed at Battlecrease House, the import of which had not been lost on the perspicacious investigative lawyer, J.H. Levy.

It was the responsibility of the Magistrates Court, not to pronounce on guilt, but to determine whether there was a case to answer in a higher court, and having considered the evidence, the Chairman of the Magistrates, Sir William Forwood, unhesitatingly committed Florence for trial on a charge of murder at the ensuing Assizes, to be held on the 31st July, in St. George's Hall, Liverpool.

When Mrs. Maybrick rose to leave the court, in order to reach the door, she had to meet full face a tier of lady spectators at the back, and the moment she turned around, the ladies started hissing her with unmistakable signs of disgust. As Mrs. Maybrick made haste to get away, the presiding justice immediately shouted at the officers on duty

to shut the door, while the burly figures of several policemen, who had made forward to the hostile spectators, effectively put an end to the outburst.
Liverpool Daily Post. 13 June 1889.

The case was now receiving coverage in the national press, and for two successive days the Lord Chamberlain, the Earl of Lathom, had been avidly following press reports of the 'Aigburth Poisoning Case', with a growing realisation of the consequences, were it ever revealed that James Maybrick, Freemason, and brother of the Grand Organist of the United Grand Lodge of England, really was Jack the Ripper.

ALICE MACKENZIE

Michael Maybrick was concerned, very concerned indeed, and rightly so. No longer was he a sole agent in charge of his own destiny on the streets of Whitechapel, but now very much dependent on the integrity of others.

Alice Yapp had become increasingly fraught as the time approached for the main trial, with the growing realisation that her spiteful contrivance could result in either Florence's execution at Walton Gaol, or Alice being publicly discredited as a liar in court, with resultant incarceration in the same prison, on a charge of perjury. A convivial meeting between her mentor and Superintendent Bryning had overcome immediate fears, and, apart from her memory lapse at the Magisterial hearing, Alice had done well so far, but the daunting County Assizes at St. George's Hall would be an entirely different matter. There, Alice would have to repeat her lies before a High Court judge with Florence only yards away, and she was deeply uncomfortable at the prospect. Edwin's nervous disposition too was becoming a potential liability. These were serious problems, which could result not only in a collapse of the prosecution case, but in Michael Maybrick's implied complicity in the death of James Maybrick.

Florence had ample time to contemplate her impending trial, but above all her thoughts were of the children, Gladys and Bobo, now in the care of Alice Yapp at Matilda Briggs's house, in the employ of Michael Maybrick, in his role as guardian under the terms of James's will. Two of the main prosecution witnesses, one of whom despised her, and the other seemingly wishing her dead, now had control over her children. Although Florence would have become aware from newspaper articles of Alice's lies at the previous hearings, there would be much at stake by implicating Alice, Edwin and more importantly Michael, with perjury at the ensuing trial. The children's welfare was of paramount importance, and Florence would have to tread very carefully in discussions with her defence barrister.

Michael Maybrick had every intention of exploiting Florence's overpowering maternal instinct to ensure her silence, but was conversely well aware that Florence would have more to gain by being proven innocent, released from prison, and re-united with her children. The fearful realisation dawned that Florence, not he, was now in control. Florence had to be silenced, and this could only be achieved by succumbing to that primal compulsion which had only been suppressed over the last eight months, sometimes with great difficulty, by avoiding his old haunts in Whitechapel. A decision was taken, even though it meant confirming Florence's suspicions that her brother-in-law really was Jack the Ripper. By 1.00 a.m. on the 17th July, Michael Maybrick was back in control.

"JACK THE RIPPER" AT IT AGAIN.

ANOTHER WHITECHAPEL TRAGEDY.

A WOMAN MURDERED AND MUTILATED IN SPITALFIELDS.

The murder fiend is at his terribly ghastly work again. Everything is on the same lines with the series of barbarous atrocities of last year, and so rarely does the crime tally with its ghastly predecessors that for all purposes we might as well tear out from the journals of that date a column or two describing one of last year's murders, alter a name here and a street there, and the sad tale would be complete. The scene of the murder is probably one of the lowest quarters of the whole of East London, and a spot more suitable for the terrible crime could hardly be found. Castle Alley. The thoroughfare is blocked up both day and night with tradesmen's carts and costermongers' barrows, and entry is by a passage no more than a yard in width leading off Whitechapel Road, entirely cut off from view of the main road, and could hardly be observed by the passer-by. The murderer, on account of the narrowness and intricacy of the surrounding thoroughfares, would have no difficulty in getting away unobserved, and if, as is believed, he is residing in one of the dozens of common lodging houses almost within a stone's throw of the spot where the deed was committed, he would have no trouble in concealing his identity, after making his escape. The woman's character, the nature of the wound, and the scene of the crime, naturally connect this murder with the seven similar murders of last year.

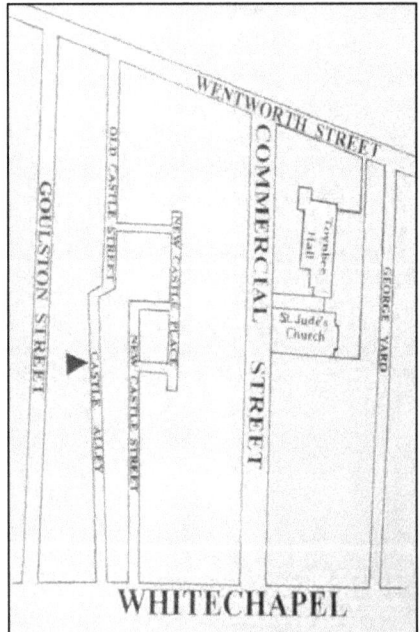

East London Observer. 20 July 1889.

Within less than a quarter of a mile of Dorset Street, where on the morning of last Lord Mayor's Day the mutilated body of Mary Jane Kelly was discovered, another brutal murder was committed on Wednesday morning, bringing up the horrible toll of Whitechapel outrages to eight. Running from Wentworth Street into Whitechapel Road is a by-alley known as Old Castle Street, which is used by costermongers of the neighbourhood for storing wheelbarrows and other miscellaneous vehicles at the close of each working day. Here, as in Mitre Square, the police patrol is timed to pass every few minutes, a circumstance which lends corroboration to the theory that this was the work of the hand which has already laid low several women of the same locality. Shortly before 1 o'clock, a constable, while passing through Castle Alley, Whitechapel, noticed a woman lying in the shadow of a doorway. He was horrified to discover she was dead, blood flowing from a wound in the throat. The wound was so deep and clean that there can be little doubt that it was inflicted by a razor or equally sharp instrument. The woman, who appeared to be about 40 years of age, lay upon her back, her clothes were turned above the waist and on the stomach an incised wound of considerable dimensions had been inflicted.

East London Advertiser. 20 July 1889.

The victim of the murder was about forty-five years of age, and was about five foot four inches in height. She had brown hair and eyes, and a fair complexion. She is believed to have been of the 'unfortunate' class, but has not yet been identified. Several hours elapsed before the woman was identified, but a man named John McCormack came forward during the day, and recognised her as Alice Mackenzie, with whom he had lived for six or seven years, and who has for some time lodged with him as his wife.

The Western Times. 18 July 1889.

A clay pipe was found next to the body, which McCormack explained as belonging to the deceased, who smoked a great deal, accounting for her street name 'Clay Pipe Alice.' Intimate knowledge of the locality was indicated by the murder scene being located on the boundary line between two police districts. Officers from Leman Street Police station, patrolling Whitechapel High Street in the course of their beat, did not enter Castle Alley, which at that end was scarcely wider than a doorway, allowing a covert vantage position from whence to assess a safe escape. Officers from Bishopsgate Police Station, on the other hand, would routinely enter from Wentworth Street at the north end of the alley, announcing their presence by the echo of hob-nailed boots, allowing ample warning for the assassin to effect a casual exit into Whitechapel High Street, while the policeman was still wending his way towards the body. Furthermore, the passageway, 180 yards in length, was dog-legged, and whilst an approaching policeman could be heard, there was no direct line of sight from Wentworth Street into the lower end of Castle Alley. A meticulously planned choice of location.

The previous evening, Alice Mackenzie had been drinking in a public house close to the Cambridge Music Hall in Commercial Street, a haunt of the balladeer Michael Maybrick, just up the road from Toynbee Hall and St. Jude's Church. There Alice was singled out, already having been shortlisted as part of the previous year's Funny Little Game, encountered in the course of patrols as a trusted member of St. Jude's Vigilance Association. With the obligatory letters 'MA' and the letter 'K' in her name, Alice may well have been on the list as the final victim of the Funny Little Game, until Mary Jane Kelly appeared on cue, bearing such an uncanny resemblance to Florence. In the assassin's eyes, Alice had simply benefited from a stay of execution. Once back in Whitechapel for the first time in months, the urge for retribution had been triggered. The uncontrollable craving for bloody retribution, the thrill of the escape, and the glory of the newspaper headlines. Euphoria.

Three days later crowds gathered, following an unrelated minor assault close to the murder scene, Screams of 'Jack the Ripper' and 'Murder', soon attracted attention, and crowds of men and women ran from all directions to the spot whence the screams proceeded. Amongst those who first arrived on the scene were several men of the local Vigilance Association, who have only just recommenced their work.

The Times. 20 July 1889.

At the inquest, held under Coroner Wynne Baxter on the morning of the 17th July, Dr. George Bagster Phillips described the wounds, including two deep lacerations to the throat, and cuts to the lower part of the body. The Coroner then stated, 'There are various points that the doctor would rather reserve at this moment,' and shortly afterwards the hearing was adjourned until mid-August. This was not the first occasion on which Dr. Bagster Phillips had been suppressing facts from the general public, including the Annie Chapman inquest, and the most outrageous of all, the inquest on Mary Jane Kelly, which had been terminated on the opening day, never to be resumed, with no evidence ever officially recorded as to the nature of the horrendous wounds inflicted. Shortly after the adjournment of the Alice Mackenzie inquest, a letter was received by the City of London Police, enclosing a small card, bearing the words 'Surely the Lord is in this House'.

A Startling Echo.
Matt. 11-12.
Sir, Will you cause these labels to be put up in a place where the woman was found dead in Whitechapel 17 inst. and it shall fulfil that the Lord has designed it to do. They are to be put up at midnight. For the Lord will look on them. Thus saith the Holy Ghost. My hand slew them. My finger stabbed them. My nails cut them in pieces. Nahum 1-2-3.'

Despite the sonorous religious overtones, Ezekiel does not receive a mention, although Nahum Chapters 1-2 were very similar in content, and had been very carefully selected,

And there is no end to their corpses, they stumble upon their corpses. Because of the multitude of their whoredoms of the well favoured harlot ... behold, I am against thee, saith the Lord of Hosts, and I will discover thy skirts upon thy face, and I will show the nations thy nakedness, and the kingdoms thy shame.

Nahum Ch. 1 – 2.

Matthew Chapter II, verse 12, cited at the top of the letter, refers directly to St. John the Baptist, patron saint of Freemasonry, celebrated just three weeks earlier, on the 24th

June at the United Grand Lodge of England, with musical celebrations orchestrated by the Grand Organist, Brother Michael Maybrick.

And from the days of John the Baptist until now the Kingdom of Heaven suffereth violence, and the violence take it by force.

Matt. Ch.11. v.12.

The enclosed card, 'Surely the Lord is in the House', may have had a dual significance in the Maybrick psyche. The opening heading to the catalogue of the Liverpool Museum of Anatomy reads, 'The House We Live In'. Was this card a souvenir, retained from his adolescent visits? Or was this a mischievous hint to the base of operations at St. Jude's Church, known only to Michael Maybrick, relishing the self-gratification of leaving yet another amusing little clue, which only he understood.

When the inquest on Alice Mackenzie was reconvened on the 14th August, Dr. Bagster Phillips continued giving evidence, and having outlined the cuts and slashes sustained, proceeded to describe a number of mysterious marks to the body, hitherto undisclosed, and very likely the reason why Dr. Bagster Phillips had adjourned the hearing four weeks earlier,

There were five marks on the abdomen, which, with the exception of one, were on the left side of the abdomen. The largest one was the lowest. They were coloured, and in my opinion were caused by the finger nails and thumb nail of a hand. I have on a subsequent examination assured myself of the correctness of this conclusion. These marks were made after the throat was cut.

During the four week period following the initial inquest, this information had remained totally confidential, leading to the obvious conclusion that the letter had been penned by the only person privy to the wounds. '*My finger stabbed them. My nails cut them in pieces.*'

Nahum 1-2-3

Within the 'Maybrick Diary' are five words which appear totally out of context, 'Oh costly intercourse of death', taken from a short work written by baroque poet Richard Crashaw (1613-1649).

Oh costly intercourse, of death and worse.
Divided love ... Quick Deaths that grow
and gather, as they come and goe.
His Nailes write swords in her, which soon her heart pays back.

Is it really coincidence that a quotation from such an obscure work as this, included completely out of context in the Maybrick Diary, should bear a remarkable similarity to the equally obscure religious wording cited in the letter posted after the Mackenzie murder, 'My finger stabbed them, my nails cut them in pieces', and to the bizarre finger nail marks on the corpse?

In Walton Gaol, Liverpool, the friendly prison warder delivered the mid-day meal to Florence Maybrick in her tiny prison cell, together with a copy of the local newspaper, in which the headline spoke volumes. Florence now knew beyond doubt that the wellbeing, possibly even the lives, of her children depended entirely on her conduct from that moment onwards. The message from Whitechapel was unspoken, but so very clear, timed as it was, only two weeks prior to Florence's trial at St. George's Hall.

In a luxurious office in Buckingham Palace, the Lord Chamberlain, personal advisor to Her Royal Majesty, Queen Victoria, threw down the latest edition of the Times, stroking his beard and mulling over the distinct possibility that the Whitechapel Murderer was still very much alive and well. Over the past few months, the Earl of Lathom had wanted to believe Michael Maybrick's contention that his brother James was the Whitechapel Murderer, and had discussed the matter informally with senior members of the judiciary, the Home Secretary, Sir Henry Matthews, and his close adviser, Permanent Under Secretary to the Home Office, Sir Godfrey Lushington. Prior to this incident, Bro. the Earl of Lathom had been convinced that Bro. Michael Maybrick may well have served the Establishment by assisting his brother James to depart this world, and that Florence was the only other party aware of her husband's involvement. This latest event could throw an entirely different light on matters, but whatever the truth, steps must be taken to dispel rumours in the press that the Whitechapel Murderer was still at large. At the resumed inquest on the 13th August, Coroner Wynn Baxter addressed Dr. Bagster Phillips, who, unsurprisingly, was intent on defraying public alarm.

Coroner: *Are the injuries to the abdomen similar to those you have seen in the other cases?*

Dr. Phillips: *No sir, I may volunteer the statement that the injuries to the throat are not similar to those in other cases.*

Coroner: *Then we have practically come to the end of the inquest.*

The Coroner's question had been deliberately side-tracked, changing the subject to a throat injury, and blatantly ignoring the query regarding the abdomen, described by an eye witness as 'an incised wound of considerable dimensions.' Dr. Bagster Phillips was clearly under instructions to toe the Establishment line. In doing so, however, he does seem to lack conviction.

'After careful and long deliberation, I cannot satisfy myself, on purely anatomical and professional grounds, that the perpetrator of the Whitechapel murders is our man.... I do not here enter into the comparison of the cases, neither do I take into account what I admit may be almost conclusive evidence in favour of the one man theory, if all the surrounding circumstance and other evidence are considered.'

Dr. George Bagster Phillips. Inquest.

Uncharacteristically, Dr. Bagster Phillips leaves a wide margin for doubt, perhaps indicating deference to his colleague, the much respected Dr. Thomas Bond, who was firmly of the opinion that the work was indeed that of Jack the Ripper, making no secret of his contention. So convinced was Dr. Bond in his interpretation of the wounds, that he had insisted on a mutual re-examination of the body with Dr. Phillips. In a letter to Assistant Commissioner Robert Anderson, Dr. Bond wrote,

I see in this murder evidence of similar design to the former Whitechapel murders, viz sudden onslaught on the prostrate woman, the throat skilfully and resolutely cut with subsequent mutilation, each mutilation indicating sexual thoughts and a desire to mutilate the abdomen and sexual organs. I am of the opinion that the murder was performed by the same person who committed the former series of Whitechapel Murders.

Dr. Thomas Bond.

As a further endorsement of Dr. Bond's opinion, Sir Charles Warren's successor, Commissioner James Monro, having examined the corpse soon after its discovery, wrote in his initial report,

I need not say that every effort will be made by the police to discover the murderer, who, I am inclined to believe, is identical with the notorious 'Jack the Ripper', of last year.

Commissioner James Munro.

Alice Mackenzie, unsurprisingly, had not been picked at random, possessing as she did the necessary MA requirement, but this choice of victim was the assassin's piece de resistance. Not only were the first nine consecutive letters of ALICE MACKENZIE included in MICHAEL MAYBRICK, but ALICE contained five of the seven letters in MICHAEL, and MACKENZIE contained five of the eight in MAYBRICK. Furthermore, as an irrefutable proof of Michael Maybrick's meticulous forward planning, the Castle Alley murder site was planned exactly on the line between Mitre Square, George Yard and Buck's Row.

Totally unaware of this clever little game, Bro. The Earl of Lathom was beginning to realise there were serious flaws in the convincingly sincere story confided in him months earlier by the Grand Organist, Bro. Michael Maybrick. James Maybrick may well be dead, but Jack the Ripper was not, and Freemasonry was still under threat from the revelation that the Whitechapel Murderer was a member of the Order.

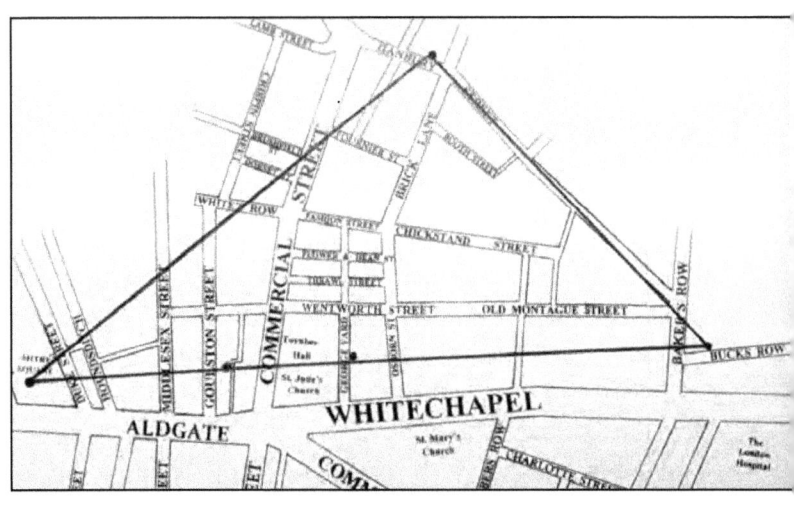

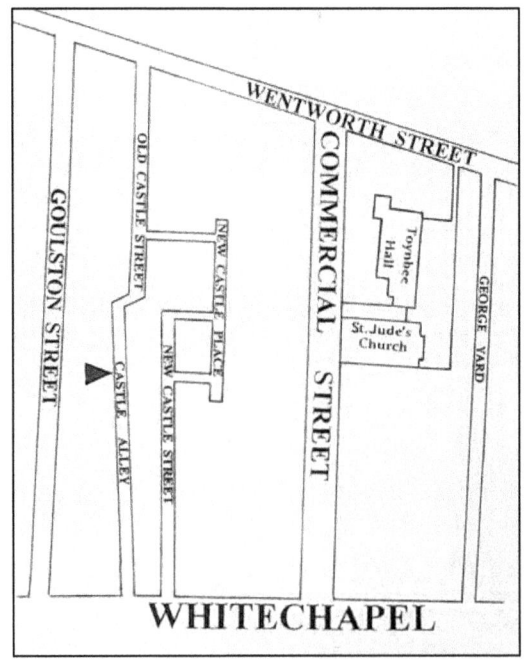

THE BLUCHER LETTER

Three months earlier, on the 29th April, just after James's stay in London with brother Michael, during which time he consulted Dr. Fuller, he wrote to Michael what has become known as the 'Blucher letter', related here again, for ease of reference.

My Dear Blucher,   *Liverpool, 29th April.*
I have been very seedy indeed. On Saturday morning I found my legs getting stiff and useless but by sheer strength of will shook off the feeling and went down on horseback to Wirral Races, and dined with the Hobsons. Yesterday morning I felt more like dying than living, so much that Florie called in another doctor who said it was an acute attack of indigestion and gave me something to relieve the alarming symptoms, so all went well until about 8 o'clock. I went to bed and had lain there one hour by myself and was reading on my back. Many times I felt a twitching but took little notice of it thinking it would pass away but instead of doing so I got worse and worse and in trying to move around to ring the bell I found I could not do so, but finally managed it but by the time Florie and Edwin could get upstairs I was stiff, and for two mortal hours my legs were like bars of iron stretched out to the fullest extent but rigid as steel. The doctor came finally again, but could not make it indigestion this time, and the conclusion he came to was that the Nux Vomica I had been taking under Dr. Fuller had poisoned me as all the symptoms warranted such a conclusion. I know I am today sore from head to feet and played out completely.

What is the matter with me? None of the doctors so far can make out, and I suppose never will until I am stretched out and cold, then future generations may profit by it if they hold a post mortem which I am quite willing they should do. I don't think I will come up to London this week, as I don't feel much like travelling and cannot go on with Fuller's physic yet a while, but I will come up again and see him shortly. Edwin does not join you just yet but he will write you himself. I suppose you go to your country quarters on Wednesday. With love,

Your affectionate brother,

Jim.

On the 3rd June, two days before the resumed inquest on the 5th, the Liverpool Courier had printed the following article, courtesy of an anonymous contributor.

ALLEGED REMARKABLE LETTER OF DECEASED
We have it upon the authority of a gentleman who affirms that he saw the document that, prior to his visit to London in April last, the late Mr. James Maybrick wrote to his brother Michael, a letter which, in view of the present circumstances, is extraordinary. The deceased gentleman said that he could not understand exactly the nature of his illness, and he thought it would be desirable, in the event of his illness proving fatal, if his body was subject to medical examination.

Liverpool Courier. 3 June 1889.

The recipient of the letter, Michael Maybrick, was the only party in a position to leak this article to the press, crucially placing on record James's suggestion of an autopsy in a letter purportedly written 'prior to his visit to London.' This was deliberate misinformation, as the letter had been written not prior to, but after James's London visit, and after James had overdosed on the London Medicine, posted to him by Michael. Furthermore, the copy letter, released to the press, deliberately omitted references in the original letter to allegations of poisoning by Dr. Fuller. Michael Maybrick had carefully cherry-picked from the original letter, securing newspaper coverage to influence public opinion, and that of the jury. Two years later, Alexander MacDougall would make a bold inference as to the article's authorship.

Now, Michael Maybrick had already given his evidence at the Coroner's inquest on the 28th May, and he certainly said nothing about having received any such letter. It would be impossible to suppose that the Liverpool Courier would have invented such a startling and sensational statement. Now I challenge the Liverpool Courier to disclose the name of the gentleman who sent the document. If Michael Maybrick really did have such a letter, he suppressed the fact when giving his evidence at the Coroner's inquest, notwithstanding the statement to which his solicitor, Mr. Steel, pledged himself, that Michael Maybrick 'wished to disclose everything he knew.' Not only was no such letter produced, but if Michael Maybrick had received it, he had kept it back from the doctors, who, if they had known of it during life, might have saved his life by administering an antidote. If Michael Maybrick really did have such a letter, it was an act of criminal suppression upon his part to keep it back from the Coroner's jury, who were sworn in, not to try Mrs. Maybrick for murder, but 'to inquire into circumstances connected with the death of James Maybrick.' Somebody, it seems to me, was very eagerly spreading false stories to prejudice the Coroner's jury against Mrs. Maybrick during the adjournment of this inquest. Who was it? And for what purpose?

Alexander MacDougall. 1891.

One day later, twenty four hours prior to the impending inquest, Michael Maybrick was once again courting the press under the guise of anonymity, free from Court restrictions, orchestrating public opinion through the columns of Liverpool's most popular daily newspaper.

In the course of an interview yesterday with a gentleman who has the case at his finger ends, one of our representatives was enabled to glean some particulars as to how the case as a whole stands so far in the minds of the prosecution. There has probably been no instance on record where the humanity and unbiased action of the police authorities have shone so conspicuously as in the Maybrick Mystery. The police superintendent has acted all through with tact, courtesy, and consideration, even kindness to Mrs. Maybrick, which in reality has its origination in the fact that the police have not taken up any strongly divided view of the case.

Liverpool Daily Post. 4 June 1889.

Having firmly established the integrity and impartiality of Michael Maybrick's new friend and prosecutor for the Crown, Superintendent Isaac Bryning, the reporter continued with reference to Florence Maybrick, instantly triggering a spontaneous and vitriolic outburst,

Our reporter put some interrogatories with a view to ascertaining what, if any, were the personal charms of Mrs. Maybrick, in the opinion of those who have come most in contact with her. He was astonished at the reply, that she had no personal charms, at least in the eye of the person who made the statement, and who has frequently seen her. In the first place, Mrs. Maybrick has that sallow, wan complexion which often marks the American, she has no great regularity of outline, and is destitute of that aristocratic skin tone which the fair sex prize so much. With the aid of the milliner and dressmaker's art, and everything desirable in the matter of personal 'make-up', as theatricals term it, Mrs. Florence Maybrick might pass in a crowd as a woman of average attraction and nothing more, even if that much.

Liverpool Daily Post. 4 June 1889.

This acerbic diatribe could well have emanated from the pen of Tobias Smollet in describing Mrs. Baynard, she of the same name as the signatory to the postcard sent to the

Whitechapel police in November, bearing five of the letters in Maybrick.

Her conversation was flat, her style mean, and her expression embarrassed. In a word, her character was totally insipid. Her person was not disagreeable, but there was nothing graceful in her address, nor engaging in her manners .... Her ruling passion was vanity, not that species which arises from self-conceit or superior accomplishment, but that which implies not even the least consciousness of personal merit.
The Expeditions of Humphry Clinker. Tobias Smollet.

The similarity in style and content not only provides a link between the author of the Baynard message and the Liverpool Daily Post informant, but gives an insight into the cynical fixation simmering within Michael Maybrick's deeply troubled mindset, containable only by avoiding 'trigger' situations. 'What are your impressions of Mrs. Maybrick?', introduced into the conversation unexpectedly, was the key to overload. The pressure was becoming increasingly difficult to contain, only manageable by avoiding the streets of Whitechapel, proof of which had come six weeks after the article, when on the 17th July, Alice Mackenzie was found butchered in Castle Alley, just off Whitechapel, a very short distance from St. Jude's Church.

THE MAYBRICK CASE

EXTRAORDINARY LETTER OF THE DECEASED

THE FRESH EVIDENCE FOR THE PROSECUTION

On the morning of the 31st July, the day on which Crown Court proceedings were due to commence, the Blucher letter surfaced yet again in the first edition of the Liverpool Daily Post, to be avidly devoured by the general public and jury members alike.

Amongst the correspondence by the deceased, Mr. James Maybrick, is a very important letter dated 29th April last, addressed to his brother Mr. Michael Maybrick, in London. In this missive, written eleven days before his death, the letter gives a minute and extremely detailed account of his mysterious illness, the first acute symptoms of which at that time began to alarm and perplex him. He states that on his returning home he was seized with a rigidity of the limbs, and a general feeling of sickness which quite prostrated him, rendering him incapable of leaving his bed. Proceeding to comment on the inability of the doctors to diagnose his complaint, he goes on to bitterly deplore their confusion of ideas, and to express an emphatic opinion that, 'this time Dr. .... cannot say that I am suffering from a violent attack of indigestion.' Towards the end of the epistle he again reverts to the strange malady that afflicts him, and adds that the medical men will perhaps be able to tell what is the matter with him when his body is cold and lifeless, and when for the benefit of future generations, they have examined his remains, a gruesome idea to which he is totally reconciled. The letter at once is pathetic and dolorous, giving a vividly startling analysis of his innermost thoughts on what he evidently anticipated was the approaching end. Whether this sensational communication will be brought before the court in the course of the trial, we are not in a position to say. But under the circumstances it casts a lurid light on the melancholy state of his mind rising from the unaccountable illness from which he is suffering at the time.

Liverpool Daily Post. 31 July 1889.

This carefully edited precis of the Blucher letter, scripted anonymously by Michael Maybrick, was even more damning than that which had conveniently coincided with the opening of the Coroner's Inquiry. The letter contains a clear inference that James was being poisoned, but blatantly omits James's suspicion that Dr. Fuller was responsible, which would have given rise to unwelcome questions being asked. The timing of this latest article was of paramount importance, leaked to a favoured newspaper reporter the previous evening, and calculated to reach the news stands on the morning of the Trial. Both these audacious moves had been carefully contrived by the Crown witness known in musical circles as Stephen Adams, and in Whitechapel as Jack the Ripper.

In the corridor of the barristers' chambers in St. George's Hall, before the opening of proceedings, a very concerned Michael Maybrick had made a bee-line for Crown Prosecutor John Addison, waving a copy of the Daily Post, as the result of which a private meeting was immediately convened with Sir Charles Russell, to discuss the implications of this controversial newspaper article. Both counsels would have read the actual Blucher letter in its entirety, alongside the spurious press article which deliberately omitted any reference to poisoning by Dr. Fuller. The real letter, soon to be produced in court, containing James's suggestion of poisoning by Dr. Fuller, would provide a damning argument for the defence. Michael Maybrick knew the letter really did substantiate a poisoned substance having been sent to James from London, and production of the Blucher letter in court would have been followed by an outright denial of this inference by Dr. Fuller, revelation of the anonymously posted London Medicine and its effects, and the serious compromise of Michael Maybrick as the only other party likely to have posted the bottle. This must not be allowed to happen. In this hastily convened meeting, Michael Maybrick would have argued that the doctor would most certainly not have prescribed lethal medicine to James, as claimed in the original letter, so why impugn the good doctors' reputation, and prejudice the reliability of his impending evidence? Much depended on the outcome of this discussion. After much deliberation, a mutual decision was taken, ironically in the interests of a fair trial, not to produce the Blucher letter in court.

SNAKE IN THE GRASS

St. Georges Hall, Liverpool.

The trial would last for seven days, the first four of which would be dedicated to evidence from the various witnesses, and the last three to addresses from the prosecution and defence, followed by the judge's summing up to the jury.

His Honour, Sir James Fitzjames Stephen, of the Queen's Bench Division, High Court of Justice, eminent historian and author on criminal law, was highly respected, with considerable judicial experience. However, two years previously he had suffered a stroke, which many considered to have affected his clarity of judgement. The life of Florence Elizabeth Maybrick was to depend very much on the judge's interpretation of the evidence as presented, his impartiality, and his final address to the jury. Herewith is a 1886 portrait of Sir James Stephen by Frederic George Watts, the very

Sir James Fitzjames Stephen, by G.F. Watts

artist whose necromantic images gazed down on the Whitechapel Murderer, as he metamorphosed back into Michael Maybrick, under the flickering candlelight in the darkness of St. Jude's Church. Seventy three days had passed since Florence's arrest at Battlecrease and incarceration in Walton Gaol, seventy three dark sunless days, seventy three long sleepless nights.

On the 31st July, 1889 the door opened from the dim corridor leading from the basement cells to the awesome splendour of the Crown Court, St. George's Hall, where all eyes gazed on the diminutive form of Florence Maybrick, emerging from the darkness.

At ten o'clock I heard a blast of trumpets that heralded the judge's entrance into the court. Accompanied by a male and female warder, I slowly ascended the stone staircase from the cell leading to the dock. I was calm and collected in manner, although aware of the gravity of my position .... Ladies were attired as for a matinee, and some had brought their luncheons that they might retain their seats. Many of them carried opera glasses, which they did not hesitate to level at me. The Earl of Sefton occupied a seat on the bench with the judge, and among the audience were many public and city men and judicial officers.

Mrs Maybrick's Own Story. Florence Maybrick.

Reassuring smiles were proffered by Florence's defence team, Sir Charles Russell QC, William Pickford and Richard Cleaver, whilst Mr. Justice James Fitzjames Stephen, bewigged and resplendent in red and ermine, stared down haughtily from on high. The press were united in commenting on Florence's composure and dignified demeanour.

Mrs. Maybrick's bearing as she stepped to the front of the dock was marked by the calmness which had made such an impression during the early stages of her terrible ordeal. She had been brought from Walton at an early hour in the prison van, in which there were several other prisoners awaiting trial. Desired to plead, she quickly said, her voice clear and musical, 'Not Guilty', and the trial was at once proceeded with. Mrs. Maybrick's somewhat protracted incarceration in Walton Gaol does not seem to have affected her health in any way. She wears black gloves, and attached to her crepe bonnet is a thin veil which falls half over her face but does not conceal it. Her dark brown hair is curled in clusters round her forehead, and without being what is regarded as classically handsome, her features are regular and pleasing, and her figure is petite and elegant.

Liverpool Mercury. 1 August 1889.

John Addison QC, in opening proceedings for the Crown, cautioned the jury against being influenced by prejudicial articles in the press, an impracticable suggestion by any stretch of the imagination, as the Maybrick Mystery had been the main topic of conversation throughout Merseyside for weeks. Unfortunately for Florence Maybrick, during previous hearings William Pickford had opted to reserve the defence, leaving the press to speculate on 'evidence' of poison and adultery, as promulgated by the Crown's bastion of law and order, Superintendent Isaac Bryning. No sooner had the address begun, than Florence's counsel, Sir Charles Russell, interrupted proceedings with a polite but extraordinary request, that with his Lordship's permission, a private discussion be convened between prosecution and defence counsels, together with the prosecution witness, Michael Maybrick. All witnesses were ushered from the courtroom, with the one exception, and a whispered conclave was held, following which Judge Stephen was advised that the Blucher letter would not be produced as evidence in court. The import of this intervention was overlooked and unreported by the press representatives in court that morning. Sir Charles Russell had unknowingly surrendered a major item of evidence for the defence, and Michael Maybrick had avoided what could have been a deeply damaging court confrontation with Dr. Fuller. The 'London Medicine' would receive only passing reference during court proceedings, and the letter would remain firmly in Michael Maybrick's inside pocket. The witnesses were duly re-admitted into the courtroom, and Mr. Addison proceeded to embark on a lengthy address to the jury.

'Gentlemen, There is no reason to doubt that what the doctors swear without doubt, that James Maybrick died by arsenic, and arsenic given to him by repeated doses. And if he did, the question will be for you, who gave him the arsenic of which he died? Undoubtedly, the whole household, whom you see, knew and had nothing to do with it. It cannot be suggested that the doctor, or his brother, or the four maidservants had anything to do with it. It will be for you to say whether the wife, who until the 8th May attended and

administered everything that was given to him through the nurses, whether she was, or was not the person who did it. It is clear that he was not a man who administered this himself by way of killing himself. The illness was attributed to an overdose of the medicine from London, to the wrong medicine being administered, to brandy, sherry, and another time, beer. There was never for one moment any notion that he was taking, in any shape or form, arsenic. Whether by the beer, the sherry, the brandy, or by the many medicines, it is clear that arsenic was being administered to him without his knowledge, or the knowledge of anyone about the place. Gentlemen, who did it? I shall be compelled, am compelled, to submit there is very cogent and powerful evidence to show that it was his wife who administered it. Undoubtedly, if she was the person who administered these repeated doses to him, then, gentlemen, she is guilty of the cruel offence of wilful murder, and it will be your painful but bounden duty to say so.

The jury was selected from outlying areas, rather than the city of Liverpool, in a misguided attempt to avoid contamination by town-centre gossip. The composition of this band of men, on whom fell the onus of interpreting the complexities of the medical evidence, does however, raise serious issues.

THE JURY

T. Wainwright	Plumber	Southport
T. Ball	Plumber	Ormskirk
A. Harrison	Woodturner	Bootle
W. Walmsley	Provision Dealer	North Meols
W. H. Gaskell	Plumber	North Meols
J. Taylor	Farmer	Melling
G. H. Welsby	Grocer	St. Helens
R. G. Brook	Ironmonger	St. Helens

J. W. Sutton	Milliner	North Meols
J. Tyrer	Painter	Wigan
J. Bryers	Farmer	Bickerstaffe
J. Thiesens	Baker	Ormskirk

The jury was subjected to Mr. Addison's persuasive rhetoric for over two hours, much of which endorsed public opinion, already prejudiced by biased articles in the popular press. Florence had no alternative but to listen in silence to Mr. Addison's denial of James's arsenic habit, and exoneration of Michael's behaviour at Battlecrease House, but displayed marked signs of discomfort as her prime accuser took to the stand.

Mrs. Maybrick betrayed a little agitation when the formula of the charge was repeated to the jury. Only once in the course of the evidence did her pallor disappear and a flush spread over her face, this being when Mr. Michael Maybrick entered the box.

Liverpool Mercury. 1 August 1889.

Was there a deeper underlying cause for Florence's concern? Was Michael Maybrick privy to personal information confided at the Café Royal, or worse, details of Florence's hidden past. Many of those present in the public gallery that day were there not only to watch the suffering of Florence Maybrick, facing a possible death sentence, but to gaze in fascination at her famous brother-in-law, prosecution witness for the Crown, and the only person in court who was fully aware of Florence's innocence. The nationally acclaimed baritone stepped forward, and, pausing for effect, addressed the hushed gathering in uncompromising stentorian tones, exuding gravitas and sincerity as he lied on oath, testimony to the duplicity which had served him so well in London.

'On Wednesday, 8th May, I left London for Liverpool. On arriving at Edgehill, I was met by my brother Edwin, and on arrival Edwin showed me a letter, dated 8th May, in the prisoner's handwriting, addressed to Mr. Brierley.'

Lie after outright lie, rendered totally credible by Michael Maybrick's imperious demeanour. The Brierley letter, now pivotal to the prosecution's case, had not even been discovered at the time of his arrival in Liverpool, and was undated. It was certainly not dated the 8th May, but by claiming the letter to have been handed over shortly after his arrival in Liverpool, Michael Maybrick instantly established justification for his otherwise inexplicable suspicion of Florence as being responsible for James's deterioration in health, and, by inference, his ultimate demise. Furthermore, deliberate reference to Florence as 'the prisoner', rather than by name, subliminally introduced an inference of guilt from the very commencement of proceedings.

The incriminating letter from Florence to Brierley was then read out to the court, but, surprisingly, the eminent defence barrister Sir Charles Russell QC; failed to pick up on either the missing date, or the anomaly present within the letter, 'both brothers-in-law are here.' Had these matters been pursued, not only would the Brierley letter have been compromised as evidence, but all three parties to the fabrication, Michael, Edwin, and Alice Yapp, would have been discredited, facing very awkward questions, and with the finger of suspicion pointing in a very different direction. Scandalously, the scheme had succeeded without the slightest hitch. Sir Charles Russell, however, was soon on the offensive.

'When you came down on Wednesday 8th May, what time did you arrive at Battlecrease?' 'At about half-past nine o'clock.' 'Where did first see your brother Edwin?' 'At Edgehill.' 'Did he then show you the Brierley letter?' 'No, he told me of it.' 'And I suppose he told you of the circumstances under which he had obtained it from the nurse Yapp?' 'Yes'. 'Tell me, I want to get at all these matters, had you from the first experience a strong suspicion in the case?' 'I did.' 'And you expressed this suspicion very openly to Mrs. Maybrick, and to the nurses?' 'No, not the nurses.' 'Did you not sir? Are you aware instructions were given to the nurses?' 'Oh, you mean the hospital nurses?' 'I said the nurses.'

What other nurses could have been the subject of the question, to prompt such a sharp denial? The only other nurse was children's nurse Alice Yapp, prime player in Michael's fabrication, prompting an uncharacteristic Freudian slip by the imperturbable Mr. Maybrick, wary of admitting any association with his protégé. Quickly regaining his composure, he continued,

'Yes, I was aware they had instructions.' 'You are aware that there were instructions given to them which would convey the idea that there was felt, by those interested in the case, considerable suspicion?' 'Yes, that is so.'

Not only were the nurses influenced by this newly introduced suspicion, so were the doctors, who, prior to Michael Maybrick's interference, would have been quite happy to issue a Death Certificate and be done with the matter, as confirmed in the cross-examination of Dr. Humphreys.

'Did it in any way never occur to you that there were symptoms present during life of arsenical poisoning? When was it that the idea was first suggested to you?' 'I think on Thursday, or on the Wednesday night, when Mr. Michael

Maybrick came to me.' 'From a communication made to you by Mr. Michael Maybrick?' 'Yes, that there was something unsatisfactory.'

The atmosphere in the court at the time of Dr. Humphreys' cross-examination is captured in the following press article.

There were a great number of fashionable females in court, many of them dressed in the loudest of summer costume. The cross gallery, high up against the roof of the court, supported by the massive grey granite columns, was filled by a line of spectators who looked like so many crows. The cross-examination of Dr. Humphreys was proceeded with quietly and monotonously, the object of Sir Charles Russell's questions appearing to be to throw doubt on the correctness of the experiments made by the doctor, and to show that he had formed his views about arsenical poisoning only after his suspicions had been aroused. Two outstanding admissions were made. Sir Charles, with quiet and calm emphasis and acute distinctiveness, asked, 'Had it not been for the suggestion of arsenic were you prepared to give a Certificate of Death?' 'Yes', answered the witness, ' If he had died on the Wednesday.' 'What was the cause of death in your judgement?' 'Acute ingestion of the stomach,' answered the doctor. ' Now,' said Sir Charles, with special deliberation and clearness, 'listen attentively and answer carefully to this question. (A pause and dead silence) Mention any post-mortem symptom which is distinctive of arsenical poisoning. (A pause) and which is not also distinctive of gastritis or gastro-enteritis inflammation of the stomach, or bowels'. 'I cannot,' answered the witness, 'I could not swear to distinguish between the two.'

Sir Charles looked triumphantly at his union counsel, and those who had closely followed the medical evidence, and understood the value of this evidence, cast meaning looks around. Liverpool Echo. 2 August 1889.

Sir Charles then turned to the subject of the Brierley letter, the existence of which had not been disclosed until the Coroner's inquest, as confirmed by Dr. Carter, Mrs. Briggs, Elizabeth Humphreys, and Mary Cadwallader. Of all the potential witnesses at Battlecrease House, only one, Dr. Richard Humphreys differed and dithered in his purported recollection.

'Now I come to Friday, the 10th, when did you first hear that the letter was intercepted by the woman Yapp?' 'I think it was on the Thursday.' 'At what time?' 'I don't know.' 'Morning or evening?' 'I cannot tell you.'
Dr. Humphreys' memory loss was suddenly on a par with Alice Yapp's. On other matters his perception had been faultless, yet on this occasion the doctor was uncharacteristically vague, possibly recalling something subsequently implanted by Michael Maybrick in the course of conversation. Dr. Carter, on the other hand, had been quite adamant at the Coroner's inquest that, prior to that hearing, no reference had ever been made to the Brierley letter, and certainly no mention of the letter had been made when the three first met on the day after Michael's arrival at Battlecrease House. Michael Maybrick had been playing mind games with Dr. Humphreys. Sir Charles next proceeded to cross-examine Dr. Carter.

'When examined by the Coroner, I want to call your attention to something you said. You said you had no idea of irritant poison until a suggestion was made to you?' 'I did.' 'Did you say in your answer to the Coroner that you didn't form an opinion that he was suffering from poison, until the suggestion was made to you?' 'That is so.'

Only once was mention made by the defence that Michael Maybrick was the originator of this mysterious undercurrent of suspicion wafting through Battlecrease House, and indeed, it seems great care was being taken not to attribute the source directly to him by name. Prior to the trial, Sir Charles Russell had engaged in prolonged discussions with Florence Maybrick in Walton Gaol. Was the eminent QC under specific instructions not to unduly malign her brother-in-law? Had the bloody message from Whitechapel left Florence in real fear for the future well-being of her children? Alice Yapp, habitual liar, and source of the damning flypaper revelation, seems to have been the only party involved who had no suspicion whatsoever.

'Did you suspect your mistress?' 'No, sir.' 'When you saw the flypapers, did you suspect her.' 'No, sir.'

Alice Yapp.

When the questioning moved on to events surrounding the bottle of Meat Juice handed to Dr. Carter by Michael Maybrick on the Friday evening, evidence was provided by Matilda Briggs's sister Martha Hughes, to the effect that she had been made aware of the presence of arsenic in the solution on the Saturday, the day of James's death. This time Michael Maybrick was named, not by Sir Charles Russell, but by Martha Hughes.

'Do you recollect hearing that arsenic was traced, and that it was found in a bottle of Valentine's Meat Juice?' 'When did you learn about the Valentine's Juice? Did you learn about that on Saturday or Sunday?' 'I heard it on Saturday.' 'Was it from Dr. Carter you heard it?' ' No.' ' From whom?' 'Michael Maybrick.'

On the Saturday, Dr. Carter had merely indicated to Michael Maybrick and Dr. Humphreys, in absolute confidence, the presence of an unknown metallic element in the bottle of Valentine's Meat Juice, which Michael had so closely monitored and handed over on Friday. It would not be until Sunday that Dr. Carter would positively confirm the presence of arsenic in the solution. The doctor had taken great care on Saturday not to mention the word arsenic, pending further tests, yet Michael, knowing full well the content, could not resist telling the sisters on the Saturday of the presence of arsenic in the bottle. Having established the point, Sir Charles Russell chose, for whatever reason, not to pursue the matter any further. Very strange, almost as though he was affirming his suspicions, but exercising a reluctant constraint. Totally unaware of the inference behind Sir Charles's line of questioning, as indeed were all onlookers, Justice James Fitzjames Stephen expressed his own views on these suspicious circumstances, totally exonerating Michael Maybrick's actions.

'If you think it for one moment, you can hardly imagine a more dreadful necessity than that of supposing that your brother's wife is carrying on a transaction of that kind. How a man could so behave, if he is unhappy enough to conceive a suspicion, how could he behave himself, and prevent himself from being reproached afterwards, either for wicked suspiciousness, or for almost criminal indulgence. The letter of Brierley certainly was grounds upon which suspicion, strong or weak, might be raised.'

Michael Maybrick's plan had succeeded. The judge was well and truly on his side. Barrister Alexander MacDougall, however, was not.

In this Maybrick case, from first to last, the question has been one of suspicious circumstances, and in dealing with it, from beginning to end, it is suspicious circumstances we have to deal with. Now suspicion itself is a nasty idea. There is, in the sound of the very word, a sibilation which reminds one of the hissing of a snake in the grass, and it is the first instinct of a healthy mind, when the word suspicion is heard, to look around and see where the word came from, to look for the snake in the grass. It is a sort of intuition which warns us, when we hear of persons being suspected, to enquire 'who suspects' and those who suspect others must expect to be suspected themselves.

Alexander MacDougall.

A REGULAR GOT-UP CASE

The first witness called on the second day of the Trial was Michael Maybrick's London physician Dr. Charles Fuller. Now the problem of the Blucher letter had been overcome, Michael could relax as his personal doctor and close friend gave evidence. Dr. Fuller was resolute that at no time did he suspect James was an arsenic addict, totally unaware that in January of that year, James had purchased enough arsenic to kill a regiment.

'I have had thirty years' experience as a practitioner. I know the symptoms which accompany the taking of arsenic. I had no reason to suppose he was taking arsenic.' 'You mean to say, then, that it was never suggested to you by anyone?' 'Never suggested by anyone.' 'No opinion has been asked of you with reference to the supposition of his having at any time taken arsenic habitually?' 'No, I have never been asked about it.'

Sir Charles Russell doggedly pursued the point, but Michael Maybrick's doctor was intent on insisting that James Maybrick was not an arsenic addict, a point more readily ingested by the jury than any amount of complex medical evidence. No reference whatsoever was made to the London Medicine.

Prior to James's death, Alice Yapp, now totally complicit in this charade of perjury and deceit, had simply intended to depose Florence, but now found herself about to be called as witness in a murder trial she had never anticipated. Despite reassurances from her mentor, this was the moment Alice had been dreading. Alice stepped forward to the witness stand, where the examination, conducted on behalf of the Crown by

Mr. John Addison QC, commenced in a friendly manner, concerning general matters within Battlecrease House, the domestic dispute after the Grand National, and the discovery of the flypapers. Alice was soon beginning to waiver, however, prompting a somewhat exasperated Mr. Addison to exclaim,

'Do try to keep up your voice. You give us a great deal of trouble.'

Alice, struggling to maintain her composure, then proceeded to contradict evidence she had provided at the earlier hearings. At the inquest Alice stated that, acting on Michael Maybrick's specific instructions, she had gone to the linen cupboard, accompanied by Bessie Brierley, to seek out a trunk, bearing Florence's initials, F.E.M.

'Whose trunk was it?' 'Mrs. Maybrick's.' 'Has it got letters on it?' 'Yes, F.E.M. on the sides.' 'What did you do with it?' 'Bessie Brierley and I took it to the night nursery.' 'What did you do with it?' 'We put it down and came out.'

Alice Yapp. inquest.

This was further indorsed at the subsequent Magisterial Hearing.

'After Mr. Maybrick's death on Saturday, I received instructions from Mr. Michael Maybrick, and in consequence Bessie Brierley and I went to the linen cupboard to get out a trunk. We took it into the night nursery, and left it there. It was marked with Mrs. Maybrick's name, and was the only one belonging to her.'

Alice Yapp. Magistrates Hearing.

Michael Maybrick's instructions were to remove this specific trunk from the linen cupboard into the children's nursery, and leave it there. No instructions to open the trunk, and no further involvement with Bessie Brierley. Now, in the Crown Court, Alice would blatantly deny that sequence of events,

'Were you instructed to look at the linen closet?' 'No, sir.' 'From what Mr. Maybrick told you, did you and Bessie go to the linen cupboard?' 'Yes.' 'What did you find?' 'We did not find anything there, but in the night nursery we found there a chocolate box and packet. They were in a trunk belonging to Mrs. Maybrick.'

Alice Yapp. Crown Court Trial.

The trunk had now mysteriously appeared in the nursery room. Sir Charles Russell appears to have overlooked these inconsistencies. The questioning continued, with Alice explaining that after a convenient lapse in time, she had brought along Nurse Wilson to be present at the opening of the case. Just why the case was not opened earlier, in the presence of Bessie Brierley, remains unanswered, but an unopened suitcase, left to order in an empty room where no-one had been allowed to enter for some time, does seem an enticing opportunity for mischief. A pre-determined plan of action appears to be emerging, as Alice continues,

'I opened the chocolate box in the presence of Nurse Wilson. She noticed the label, 'Arsenic. Poison for Cats'. I observed a handkerchief in the box, with two bottles underneath.' ' Do you know whose handkerchief it was?' 'It was Mrs. Maybrick's.'

How convenient that independent witness Nurse Wilson, who had no business in the children's nursery, should be present at the 'discovery', and that Nurse Wilson, not Alice Yapp, should notice the label, 'Poison. Arsenic for Cats.' How convenient also, that according to Alice, alongside the arsenic, in a suitcase clearly marked 'F.E.M.', should be found a handkerchief belonging to Florence Maybrick. Truly incriminating evidence, yet hardly the place where a scheming murderess would hide deadly poison, directly implicating herself in the crime. How unfortunate that Nurse Wilson's evidence at the inquest some weeks earlier directly contradicts Alice's claim. Alice had underestimated the perceptive abilities of a nurse trained to pay attention to detail.

'I was present when the trunk was opened, and saw all the things taken out of it. I did not notice any handkerchief.'
Nurse Wilson. inquest.

The strange circumstances surrounding the discovery of the suitcase and its contents were then unaccountably dropped by Sir Charles Russell, another missed opportunity to delve deeper into the motivation behind Alice's unaccountable involvement in a seemingly staged event. Michael Maybrick's input into the arrangements was inexplicably disregarded, ignored, and instead Sir Charles opted to change tack, intent on disparaging not only Alice's credibility, but her trustworthiness.

'About the question of the flypapers. Have you ever acted as a lady's maid?' 'No, only as a nurse.' 'Was it in the morning that Bessie Brierley told you as to having seen the flypapers?' 'No sir, it was soon after dinner.' 'And you, out of curiosity, went into the room after dinner was over?' ' Out of curiosity?' 'Yes'. 'You had no business in the room?' 'No'.

Alice had been snooping around, a source of deep concern for all onlookers in court that day, as nearly all would have engaged domestic staff, with the possible exception of the jury members. Alice could not be trusted. Was her evidence reliable? Could she be believed? With Alice on the back foot, Sir Charles then turned to the subject of the Brierley letter.

'Now, with regard to this letter, you had heard the name of your mistress coupled with the name of Brierley before you got the letter?' ' Never.' 'Why did you open the letter?' 'Because Mrs. Maybrick wished it to go by that post.' 'Why did you open that letter?' (No reply).

Mr. Justice Stephen: 'Did anything happen to that letter?'

'Yes, it fell in the dirt, my lord.' 'Why did you open that letter?' 'I have answered you, sir.'

Mr. Justice Stephen: ' She said because it fell in the dirt.'

'With great deference to your lordship, she did not say so. Your lordship is referring to something before.'

Mr. Justice Stephen: 'She has just said so now.'

'Well, I did not catch it. Anyway, I want to have it out again. Why did you open that letter?' 'I opened the letter to put it in a clean envelope.' 'Why didn't you put it in a clean envelope without opening it?' (No reply). 'Was it a wet day?' ''It was showery.' 'Are you sure of that?' 'Yes.' 'Will you undertake to say that? I ask you to consider. Was it a wet day?' (No reply). 'Aye or no?' (No reply). 'Was it a wet day or a dry day?' (No reply). Had the day before been a dry day?' 'It was showery.' 'Will you swear that on Wednesday it was showery?' 'I cannot say positively.' 'Let me see the letter. Just take the envelope in your hand. Is the direction clear enough?' 'It was very much dirtier at the time.' 'It hasn't obscured the direction, which is plain enough?' 'No.' 'If, as you suggest, this fell in the mud and was wet, there is no running of the ink?' 'No, sir.' 'Can you suggest how there can be any damp or wet in connection with it, without

causing some running of the ink?' 'I cannot.' 'On oath girl, did you manufacture that stain as an excuse for opening your mistress's letter?' 'I did not.' 'Have you any explanation to offer about the running of the ink?' 'I have not.' 'I put it to you again for the last time. Did you not open the letter deliberately, because you suspected your mistress?' 'No sir, I did not.'

Alice Yapp had been exposed as an unconvincing and untrustworthy liar, but nothing of any significance had been proved. Sir Charles Russell knew Alice was lying, but was not to know that the whole tale had been based on an event which had occurred days before, hence Alice's uncertainty over the weather on the Wednesday. So what did Mr. Justice James Fitzjames Stephen have to say about Alice Yapp's evidence?

'This is a letter on which so much turns. Sir Charles Russell asked several times whether she did not drop the letter in the mud in order to make an excuse to open it afterwards. Whether her object was not to intercept the correspondence, I don't think it makes the smallest difference to Mrs. Maybrick's guilt or innocence, but I should be sorry if a woman, who seemed to be well spoken and respectable, should commit wilful and corrupt perjury.'

It makes all the difference in the world, your lordship, it makes the difference between life and death. Is it right that the equally 'well spoken and respectable' Florence Maybrick should be executed on the strength of the 'wilful and corrupt perjury' of Alice Yapp?

Alexander MacDougall, retired barrister, had called on the favour of colleagues to ensure a seat in the courtroom on every day of the Trial, and, whilst it would be two years before he would commit his thoughts to print, they graphically represent his frame of mind at that time, from the moment Alice Yapp approached Mrs. Briggs in the garden.

Alice Yapp gave birth to the suspicions of arsenic on the morning of Wednesday 8th May, and adultery in the afternoon of the same day. But my readers will not believe that suspicions of such a nature as these grow, like mushrooms, in a day, My readers will entertain no doubt that there is something behind all this, that there was some wire puller behind the scenes. Who can answer the question which is the real mystery of the Maybrick case? How, why, and by whom was the charge of murdering her husband put upon Mrs. Maybrick?

Alexander MacDougall.

MacDougall had not been taken in by Michael Maybrick's posturing, knew very well how, why and by whom, false evidence had been contrived, but just couldn't understand the motive.

Nurse Gore, in the course of cross-examination, then relayed the sequence of events surrounding the bottle of Valentine's Meat Juice, surreptitiously introduced by Edwin Maybrick on the evening of Michael's arrival at Battlecrease House.

'I gave Mr. Maybrick some of the Valentine's Meat Juice. Mr. Edwin Maybrick had given me the bottle on the Wednesday night. I gave him one or two teaspoonfuls in water ... Mrs. Maybrick passed through the bedroom, and in doing so she took the bottle from the chest of drawers. She went into the dining room, and remained there about two minutes...'

Sir Charles continued probing, intent on proving that James's deterioration could not be attributed to interference with the Valentine's Meat Juice by Florence.

'To the best of your opinion, observation and knowledge, Miss Gore, was anything injurious given to the patient during any of your watches' 'Not that I am aware of.' 'Now I wish to speak about the bottle of Meat Juice. Was it a full bottle?' 'Yes.' 'Now you have told us of seeing the bottle removed. The bottle was taken away by Mrs. Maybrick to the next room. And it perhaps would not be too much to say that your suspicions were aroused?' 'Yes.' 'Very well, your suspicions being aroused, you took great care not to give it to the patient?' 'Yes.' 'You are clear on that point?' 'Yes'.

In the course of the first four days of the trial, a further forty two witnesses would be called, including household servants, chemists, nurses, and police officers. Statements were provided by parties privy to James's habit of dosing himself with harmful substances, but apart from his intake years earlier, whilst in Virginia, no direct reference was made to arsenic. Unconvincing attempts were also made to justify Florence's use of flypapers as a cosmetic, but no attempt was made to source substantiation of the practice in America or Europe. Nor was Florence's mother called as a witness, despite later assurances that she had been fully prepared to endorse in detail Florence's use of arsenic as a cosmetic.

Of crucial significance, if, as alleged by the prosecution, Florence Maybrick had been in possession of a secret stache of arsenic in Battlecrease House, why on earth would she have gone to the trouble of soaking fly-papers? At no time did Sir Charles Russel pursue this powerful case for the defence.

The unfolding saga leading to James's deterioration in health was then pursued, leading to Florence's arrest, and the subsequent search for incriminating material. Household gossip sustained the interest of all present as matrimonial problems were revealed, leading up to that event for which all were awaiting. Details of the dalliance at Flatman's Hotel had already been revealed at the inquest, but, whatever the legal aspects of the case, this was still the subject which galvanized public interest, sold newspapers, and swayed opinions.

Alfred Schweisso was called to the stand, once again singing out his damning evidence of adultery at the London hotel, followed by testimony from Inspector Richard Baxendale, relating his personal discovery of incriminating items at Battlecrease, most of which had been unearthed not by him, but by Michael Maybrick's personal assistants, who had been allowed to roam free over the crime scene.

Six months later, in January 1890, barrister Alexander MacDougall received the following letter from Alfred Schweisso, the star witness who had claimed to identify Florence and Alfred Brierley, during their weekend in Flatman's Hotel, London, which so swayed public opinion against the adulteress Florence Maybrick.

66 Oliphant Street
Queen's Park Estate
London   January   18th,
1890.

I received your letter this morning at this address where I am staying, as I have left Flatman's. I should be too glad to do that which would be of assistance in getting Mrs. Maybrick released. I am aware that everybody for the prosecution was dead against her, especially those whose duty was to go no further than seeing that justice was done, but they proved to me to be two-faced. I am really sorry to say that I did not act as I ought to have done, inasmuch as it was a matter of life and death, but I was really afraid of the consequences that might happen. I will give you an instance. When I arrived at the Coroner's inquest, I met an Inspector. This was the conversation that passed between us. He said, 'Will you be able to recognise Mrs. Maybrick?' I said I should not. He said, 'Keep with me and I will take you so as you can see her, because you will be sworn whether you can recognise her or not when you are called.' I saw her twice before I was taken to recognise her to the order of the Coroner.

Secondly, I had more trouble in recognising Mr. Brierley. He was in the court all the morning, near where I was standing myself, and I did not recognise him. The Inspector came to me again, and said, 'Mr. Brierley was against you, I suppose you recognised him?' Well, I never saw him. I give you this statement to show you that honestly I could not recognise him if it had not been for the police. You are aware that the Coroner dealt chiefly on Mrs. Maybrick's movements in summing up, and that it was published in the local papers that it would be quashed up. I told the Inspector this. He said, 'I have seen it myself, but I have a different opinion, for it's going to end against her.' Now, with regard to Mr. Brierley, of course I should not have recognised him at all if it had not been for the police, but as I was for the prosecution, I went by their orders, which I am sorry for now, for they acted in a very shameful manner. Well, after they returned from luncheon, that Inspector told me to nod to him when I recognised Brierley, as he would be in court in two or three minutes. Well, I could not recognise him when he came, but a policeman came up to me, and showed me where Mr. Brierley was. I give you this statement voluntarily to show you, as far as I am concerned, that it was a regular got-up case of the police.

Yours faithfully

Alfred Schweisso.

Alexander MacDougall.

Not only had Inspector Baxendale, and by inference Superintendent Bryning, acted feloniously in inducing Schweisso to commit perjury, but had confided that the outcome of the inquest was already decided, a sentiment evidently shared by Coroner Brighouse. Michael Maybrick, by carefully remaining in background, had managed once again to remain invisible.

A word of praise is due to Superintendent Bryning, not only for the succinct and indefatigable way in which he laid his evidence before the jury, but for the skilful manner in which he examined and re-examined the various witnesses whom he called. He was quite equal to the occasion, and the best proof of his ability consisted in the fact that he left not the slightest loophole for the learned counsel arranged against him.

Liverpool Daily Post. 28 May 1889.

THE MISSING PILL BOX

Doctors Humphreys and Carter had already testified that, without Michael Maybrick's interference, death would have been diagnosed as gastro-enteritis, and a Death Certificate duly issued. It would now be the turn of the medical experts to voice their opinions. The line-up was as follows,

Prosecution

Dr. Thomas Stevenson	Home Office Analyst.
Mr. Edward Davies	County Analyst.
Dr. Alexander Barron	Prof of Pathology. Liverpool University.

Defence

Dr. Charles Tidy	Examiner of Forensic Medicine. London University.
Dr. Rawdon MacNamara	Doctor of Medicine. Liverpool University.
Professor Ralph Paul	Prof of Medicine. Liverpool University.

All agreed that death had been due to acute irritation of the stomach, but there was a pronounced conflict of opinion as to whether or not the cause had been arsenic. Oddly, at no stage in proceedings was it suggested that strychnine could have been responsible. Both prosecution and defence counsels displayed commendable in-depth knowledge of the medical intricacies which divided the experts, with evidence produced over many hours, based on selected samples chosen to support individual theories, involving calculations based on thousandths of a grain of arsenic. The outcome was endless rhetoric, resulting in an unconvincing stalemate, well beyond the understanding of the working men of the jury. If the intellectual capacity of this group were cause for concern, the situation would be compounded by a statement later provided by court official, Mr. Arthur Dones.

'I was in Liverpool, in the ordinary course of professional business, and stayed at the Victoria Hotel. The day previous to the verdict, I went to the billiard room of the Imperial, about 120 yards from the Victoria. I saw there several of the jurymen who were on the Maybrick case. I recognised them as I was in Court each day of the trial. There were five or six jurymen present, two of whom were playing billiards, and there were three or four sitting down talking to the general public. There were eight or ten people present, besides the jurymen. The conversation turned upon the Maybrick case, and I have no doubt the jurymen heard the observations made by the public present. I remarked to a fellow clerk on Circuit what an odd thing it was that the jury should be allowed to mix with the public. The conversation about Mrs. Maybrick was in ordinary tones, without any disguise, and I have not the slightest doubt but that the jurymen heard nearly everything that was passing. What struck me as extraordinary was that the jury should have been allowed to walk the streets from one hotel to another, the newspapers boys passing along, calling out the news. It is the practice that juries be locked up, and, if they want an airing, they generally go in a closed carriage. I never remember such a case. In the billiard room I noticed the bailiff, but he took no precautions, letting the members of the jury mix with the people without expostulation.'.

Alexander MacDougall. 1891.

The medical experts had spoken, and no-one was any the wiser. In the witness gallery, Edwin Maybrick, bored as everyone else that afternoon, was suddenly jolted out of his reverie as Sir Charles Russell took to the floor, brandishing a pill-box, which was all too familiar to Edwin. Holding the box on high, Sir Charles addressed the court.

'I would like to call someone, my lord, to speak to a box I have here, which is labelled Taylor Brothers, Pharmaceutical Chemists, Norfolk, Virginia, and the description of the contents of which says, 'Iron quinine and arsenic, one capsule every three or four hours. At the bottom of it is the name Mr. Maybrick.'

The pill box, held by Sir Charles Russell, had mysteriously appeared amongst the court exhibits. Mr. Addison immediately indicated his intention to call Edwin Maybrick, whereupon Sir Charles interjected, stating that he would not be pursuing the irregularity of the matter. Why not? Edwin had been tampering with court evidence, and was about to be forced to admit to it. A clearly shaken Edwin Maybrick took to the stand.

Sir Charles:	*I do not wish to make any complaint about this not being produced by anyone.*
Mr. Addison:	*Is it on the printed list?*
Sir Charles:	*It is not.*
Mr. Addison:	*Mr. Edwin Maybrick will tell us all about it. Where did you find this box?*
Edwin Maybrick:	*I found it in the drawer of the washstand in my brother's bedroom.*

Mr. Addison:	It is dated Norfolk, Virginia. How long is it since he was there?
Edwin Maybrick:	Since 1884.
Mr. Addison:	Was that the last time he was there?
Edwin Maybrick:	Yes.
Sir Charles:	Do you know how this escaped being recorded amongst the things found?
Edwin Maybrick:	I found it at the time the furniture was removed from the house.
Sir Charles:	Did you know that Mr. Cleaver, President of the Law Society was acting for the lady?
Edwin Maybrick:	I did.
Sir Charles:	Did you communicate it to him?
Edwin Maybrick:	No.
Sir Charles:	What did you do with it?
Edwin Maybrick:	I kept it.
Sir Charles:	When did you first give it?
Edwin Maybrick:	On the 1st August.

Sir Charles Russell had Edwin at his mercy, but, inexplicably, let the matter drop. Edwin had been in possession of the pill-box since, at the very least, the 25th May, yet two weeks later, at the inquest on the 6th June, Edwin had stated categorically that he had no knowledge of James's drug habits. Furthermore, an affidavit given on oath by family friend Captain Peter John Irving some months after the trial, does confirm Edwin's knowledge of James's strychnine habit.

'I was well acquainted with the deceased James Maybrick and with his brother Edwin. I remarked in the course of the

evening how unwell the deceased then appeared, and mentioned the circumstance afterwards to his brother Edwin, who in reply stated to me that it was in consequence of the poison he was taking. I enquired what poison he was taking and he replied strychnine.'

Captain Peter Irving.

Why would Edwin have been so foolish as to illicitly introduce the pill-box into the court exhibits? Or could it have been Michael, not Edwin, who had purloined certain items from Battlecrease House, and hidden them in James's office, where Edwin was still conducting business, assisted by clerks George Smith and Thomas Lowry. Were items discovered by Lowry, and brought to Michael's attention? Does this explain the following passage in the Maybrick Diary?

'If I could have killed the bastard Lowry with my bare hands there and then I would have done so. How dare he question me on any matter, it is I that should question him. Damn him, damn him, damn him. Should I replace the missing items? No, that would be too much of a risk. Should I destroy this? My God I will kill him? Give him no reason and order him poste haste to drop the matter, that I believe is the only course of action I can take. I will force myself to think of something more pleasant.'

The Diary of Jack the Ripper. Shirley Harrison.

Had Bro. Sir Charles Russell been tactfully notified of this 'oversight' by Bro. Michael Maybrick on the day of Edwin's first court appearance? If Thomas Lowry had indeed discovered the incriminating pill-box, Michael Maybrick would have been obligated to raise the matter with Sir Charles Russell, who for whatever reason, opted to discreetly avoid raising the issue there and then, instead bringing the matter to light at the end of the witness hearings, emphasising that he had no intention of lodging an official complaint. Tampering with court evidence is a criminal offence, but, courtesy of Sir Charles Russell, the matter was not pursued, and Judge James Fitzjames Stephen said nothing. All very odd. The fact remains, Edwin, or Michael, had deliberately withheld the pill-box from Florence's defence lawyer, and Sir Charles Russell had unaccountably and single-handedly determined that this serious misdemeanour merited no further action, almost as though he was going out of his way to remain in favour with Michael Maybrick. However, the court of public opinion, and, of paramount importance to Edwin, his colleagues in the Cotton Exchange, would not be so forgiving.

Once all the witnesses had been heard, Sir Charles Russell addressed Florence Maybrick, enquiring whether she wished to make a statement, the only occasion on which a prisoner was allowed to address the court. In faltering tones, aided by notes, Florence proceeded to explain her cosmetic use of arsenic and elderflower solution in Europe and America, and how fly-papers had proved an effective alternative. Then, changing the subject to the Valentine's Meat Juice, Florence admitted to complying with James's instructions to add powder to the solution on the night of the 8th May,

'I went and sat on the bed beside him. He complained to me of being very sick and very depressed, and he implored me to give him this powder, which he had referred to earlier in the evening and which I had declined to give him. I was overwrought, terribly anxious, miserably unhappy, and his evident distress utterly unnerved me. He had told me that the powder would not harm him, and that I could put it in his food. I then consented. My lord, I had not one true friend in

that house. I had no-one to consult, and no-one to advise me. I was deposed from my position as mistress in my own house, and from attending my own husband, notwithstanding that he was so ill. I removed the bottle from the small table, where it would attract his attention, to the top of the washstand, where he could not see it. There I left it, my lord, until, I believe, Mr. Michael Maybrick took possession of it.'

Michael did indeed take possession of the bottle, but not until Nurse Callery's watch the following day, to be substituted by one of his own. Florence's statement was met by silence in the courtroom, as whilst those present seemed to relate to her honest naivety, it was evident that Florence had prejudiced her defence by clouding matters even further with regards the Valentine's Meat Juice.

The vein of pleading and repentance which ran through it was impressively touching.
Liverpool Mercury. 6 August 1889.

Counsels for the defence and prosecution would next spend five long hours addressing the jury, during which time the oratorial skills of Sir Charles Russell were put to the test, convincingly expounding lines of argument to establish reasonable doubt as grounds for acquittal. Mr. John Addison, whilst pressing home circumstantial evidence in support of conviction, was commendably magnanimous in the course of his address, whilst adhering to his remit as counsel for the prosecution.

'These are the salient points in this case. If, after considering those, you find the case not made out, if a strong doubt remains as to her guilt, then I hope you will act upon it, and it will afford much gratification to many people if you acquit her upon such a ground as that. You would only be carrying out the law, which says you must be satisfied of a prisoner's

guilt. It is only in case of your minds being firm and clear that I would suggest that you should find this prisoner guilty. If she is guilty, and you are satisfied, we have indeed by this investigation brought to light a very terrible deed of darkness, and a murder founded on profligacy and adultery, carried out with such a hypocrisy and cunning rarely equalled in the annals of time.'

On Tuesday, the sixth day of the trial, Judge Stephen embarked on a marathon address to the jury which would last twelve hours, until the next day. The effects of his recent stroke were manifested on a number of occasions in the course of this tedious dialogue, resulting in undisguised exasperation of both defence and prosecution advocates. Mistakes were made in dates, facts and figures.

Judge Stephen:	*The next date is the Grand National something. I don't know whether it is a race, or a steeplechase, or what it is, but it is something that is called the Grand National.*
Judge Stephen:	*Somewhere about the 12th to 19th March took place the purchase of flypapers .....*
Mr. Pickford:	*Will your lordship forgive me? The dates were the 24th and 29th April, not March.*
Judge Stephen:	*I said April. There is no use disputing whether I used one word or the other.*

Opposing barristers engaged raised eyebrows, as conjecture replaced fact, with the judge's monotone inducing the tedium which had pervaded the court during the previous day's medical evidence, and offering no guidance whatsoever to the befuddled members of the jury.

'The evidence of a number of medical men, 'I think he died of arsenic poisoning', or 'I don't think he died of arsenic poisoning, but of gastro-enteritis,' may be passed over as more fit for medical jurisprudence than for a jury engaged upon the administration of criminal law .... the mere fact of a man swearing this, that, and the other does not by any means give a reason for unqualified belief in what he says. The doctors are divided in opinion, and, of course, I cannot answer the question whether there was arsenic poisoning or not.... I do not wish to say anything definite about it, but you have formed your own opinion as to their impartiality, their partisanship, their knowledge generally. I am very sorry I can do so little to help you in this great matter, but it is great relief to me that, under the constitutional law of this country, it is you who have to decide the case, and not I, and all I have a right to do is to call your attention to the different matters in the case. I am sorry to say that I must require your attention tomorrow at the usual hour of ten o'clock.'

Having arbitrarily discredited the reliability of the medical witnesses, Judge Stephen then proceeded to abrogate his judicial responsibility, by expecting the intricacies of the case to be interpreted, without guidance, by a jury of laymen which he had just determined as being not fit for purpose. Despite the judge's ramblings, the general consensus of opinion was that reasonable doubt had definitely been established, and, for the first time, Sir Charles Russell felt reasonably assured of an acquittal. The scurrying of jury members to the public bar of the Imperial Hotel was not reported, but is not in doubt. A fellow American, Dr. Helen

Densmore, avidly pursuing events, had her own views on proceedings,

'It is a great grief and scandal that a question of life and death, too intricate to be decided by the knowledge of those who know all that is to be known on the subject, should be remitted to the ignorance of those who know nothing. It is an unheard of grief and scandal, and a menace to life and liberty, that a jury of three plumbers, two farmers, one woodturner, one provision dealer, one grocer, one ironmonger, one milliner, one painter, and one baker, who, however honest and intelligent, are necessarily not experts in metaphysics, should be instructed by the judge to turn away from the evidence which acquits the prisoner, and to turn inward to their own metaphysics for a verdict that convicts to death'.

Dr. Helen Densmore. The Maybrick Case. 1892.

It is not on record where Judge Stephen resided during the Trial, but his coach arrived and left Liverpool every day by way of London Road, in the direction of the Earl of Sefton's estate on the outskirts of Liverpool, where a safe haven would have been assured. The Earl of Sefton had been on the Judge's Bench every day, in his official capacity as Deputy Lieutenant of Lancashire, and was an adjoining landowner to the Earl of Lathom in West Lancashire, and fellow member of the House of Lords.

Had the Earl of Lathom confided in the Earl of Sefton, expressing the implications for national security, and consequential repercussions within the Establishment, should Florence be allowed to publicly voice her inside information on the Whitechapel Murderer? Were those sentiments communicated that very evening by the Earl of Sefton to Judge Stephen, prior to his final address to the jury? The following passage is taken from a book written by Sir Henry Fielding Dickens, K.C., barrister-at-law, Inner Temple, London, relating to the observations of a fellow judge residing in the same premises as Judge Stephen that evening.

He summed up all day, apparently in favour of Mrs. Maybrick, and adjourned the remainder of what he had to say until next morning. That night his brother judge had a somewhat startling experience. Early in the morning he was awakened by Stephen, whom he found walking up and down in his room, saying as he did so, 'That woman is guilty. That woman is guilty.' He continued his summing up next day, but in a manner altogether opposed to what he had said on the previous day.

Memories of my Father: Charles Dickens. Sir Henry Fielding Dickens.

DAY OF JUDGEMENT

Wednesday, 7th August, was the final day of the Trial, and, with the life of Florence Elizabeth Maybrick hanging in the balance, Judge Stephen spent the whole morning expounding on the intricacies of the medical evidence, creating reasonable doubt in the minds of all concerned, if only due to a total lack of understanding of what he was saying.

You have heard all that has been said, and all that could be said, upon a considerable variety of subjects, and now I am about to say that the facts are not always fair, which is meant to sound very surprising. The danger against which I wish to warn you is this, that as soon as you are told that a particular circumstance takes place in connection with a great trial of this kind, as soon as any circumstance associated with such a trial as this occurs, it is a natural tendency of the human mind to separate it from common things, and to say that this is a part of the evidence that we are to look upon as a very serious matter, as a thing which has been brought forward, sorted out and set before us in order, because it is an element in the case ....

Was Judge Stephen really in full control of his faculties? Nobody could possibly interpret the meaning, let alone the relevance of such endless diatribe, yet the judge continued in similar vein throughout the morning, displaying signs that he had not fully recovered from the stroke he had recently suffered. Years later, the situation was summed up by an article in the Liverpool Daily Post.

THE GREAT MAD JUDGE

'Few who looked upon the strong square head can have suspected that the light of reason was burning very low within. Yet as the days of the Trial dragged by, men began to nod, to wonder, and to whisper. Nothing more painful was

ever seen in court than the proud old man's desperate struggle to control his failing faculties. But the struggle was unavailing. It was clear that the volume of facts was unassorted, undigested in his mind; that his judgement swayed backwards and forwards in the conflict of testimony; that his memory failed to grip the most salient features of the case for many minutes together. It was shocking to think a human life depended upon the direction of the wreck of what was once a great judge.'
Liverpool Daily Post. 13 August 1900.

After a mid-day adjournment, Judge Stephen returned to court fully invigorated, with a very different, meaningful agenda. Could this have been the result of a further discussion over lunch with Lord Sefton, anxious to implement the edicts of the Lord Chamberlain? In a supposedly impartial summing-up, Judge Stephen embarked on a mission to directly link Florence to the stache of arsenic in Battlecrease House, simply because it was on the premises.

There is evidence about a considerable quantity of poison in the house. .... It was poison of which it might be said with certainty Mrs. Maybrick had access. It is very difficult indeed to have to suggest any reason why an ordinary person should require that quantity of arsenic in that kind of state, and I find a difficulty in finding words moderate enough, but I should say that a person is somewhat unfortunately situated, being supposed to have been guilty of poisoning her husband with such a large quantity of arsenic distributed, at the time when it was suggested that she did commit so horrible a crime.

Having done his level best to associate Florence with husband James's personal stache of arsenic, Judge Stephen then proceeded to condemn Florence on the strength of her proven adultery with the scoundrel Brierley, the one subject that the jurymen would actually understand. No more impartiality, rather a vitriolic outburst worthy of a prosecution barrister, tantamount to an indictment of Florence's guilt.

I feel that it is a dreadful thing that you are deliberately considering, whether or not you are to convict that woman of really as horrible, as dreadful a crime as any poor wretch who stood in the dock was accused of .... For a person to go deliberately administering poison to a poor, helpless sick man, upon whom she had already inflicted a dreadful injury, an injury fateful to married life, the person who could do such a thing must indeed be destitute of the least trace of human feeling .... it seems horrible, to comparatively ordinary people, that a woman should be plotting the death of her husband in order that she might be left at liberty to follow her own degrading vices. I will not say anything about it, except that it is easy enough to conceive how a horrible woman in so terrible a position might be assailed by some fearful and terrible temptation.

At the conclusion of Judge Stephen's twelve hour address, the jury retired to consider their verdict. This would normally be a time consuming exercise extending over a period of hours, but in this instance the twelve men took precisely forty three minutes to officially confirm the decision informally determined at the bar of the Hotel Victoria on the previous evening.

The jury returned at four minutes to four, and the whole of the persons in court rose and stood in silence. The silence and the tension of the moment was most impressive. After being asked by the Clerk of Arraigns whether they found the prisoner guilty or not guilty, the foreman of the jury pronounced the verdict in a low voice, 'Guilty'. After an instant's hush there was a loud murmur, half a groan, and half an expression of astonishment, but it was mostly decidedly expressed and felt throughout the court, and during the following few moments of the pronouncement there were few who were not shaken with the pain and agitation of the terrible scene. At the moment of the verdict, the prisoner dropped her head down on one hand, resting it almost on her knee, and sat in that attitude for about fifteen seconds amid the profoundest silence.

Liverpool Echo. 8 August 1889.

Judge Stephen donned the black cap, and without commenting on the verdict, proceeded to pass sentence.

'Prisoner at the bar. I am no longer able to treat you as being innocent of the dreadful crime laid at your charge. The jury have convicted you, and the law leaves me no direction, and I must pass on you the sentence of the law. This Court doth ordain you to be taken from the place whence you came, and from thence to the place of execution, and that you there be hanged by the neck until you are dead, and that your body be afterwards buried within the precincts of the prison in which you shall have been confined after your conviction, and may the Lord have mercy on your soul.'

Michael Maybrick, watching expressionless, was quietly exuberant. In three weeks' time Florence Maybrick would be dead, his secret would be safe, and he would be covertly lauded within the higher echelons of Freemasonry and the Establishment. Perhaps he would indeed receive the knighthood which he considered his entitlement, followed by a commission in oils by Frederic George Watts.

MR. R.F. MUCKLEY

Michael's reveries were to be short-lived, blurred by murmurings of dissention throughout the court within seconds of the sentence having been passed, followed by a seismic reaction from the crowd outside.

At this juncture the jury were about to be discharged, and, as they stood up, loud hisses were heard. When the verdict became known outside, there were loud groans and hooting from a very large portion of the immense multitude that had assembled, and there were several scenes of a very exciting character, almost everyone who came out of the building being subjected to unpleasant scrutiny and enquiry. But the greatest scene of all occurred upon the departure of Mr. Justice Stephen. When the judge's carriage drew up, the crowds surged in that direction until the street near the end of London Road became almost impassable. When the judge entered the carriage it drove rapidly off, and was followed for a considerable distance by a crowd of a thousand or more, who hooted in the most vehement and unmistakable manner.

Birmingham Daily Mail. 8 August 1889.

> ## THE MAYBRICK MYSTERY.
>
> GREAT OUTBURST OF POPULAR INDIGNATION IN LIVERPOOL.
>
> JUSTICE STEPHEN DEPARTS AMID A STORM OF GROANS
>
> MRS. MAYBRICK CHEERED BY THE CROWD.

In direct contrast, Florence's reception on being driven away from St. George's Hall, was ecstatic. Alice Yapp and Matilda Briggs were jostled by the crowd, and only with police assistance were they were able to take refuge in a nearby hotel. Albert Schweisso made it as far as Lime Street Station en route to the next train back to London, only to have two teeth unceremoniously knocked out by an irate member of the mob. Unsurprisingly, Michael Maybrick, with Edwin in tow, managed to slip away unnoticed, an art which he had mastered to perfection.

A crowd of several hundred persons assembled at the south end of St. George's Hall a little before six o'clock last evening, in order to see the departure of Mrs. Maybrick for Walton Gaol. About six o'clock the gates were thrown suddenly open, and the prison van containing Mrs. Maybrick emerged from the gateway, and was driven away at a rapid trot. The crowd of people was obviously in sympathy with Mrs. Maybrick, and as the prison vehicle, black and melancholy, drove through the streets en route to Walton, it was cheered and cheered to the echo by thousands of persons.

Liverpool Daily Post. 17 August 1889.

The trial was now the focus of national concern, stirred by the enormity of the death sentence passed on a woman believed by most not to have been proven guilty. Open criticism was expressed by the judiciary and the medical profession, the latter particularly incensed at Judge Stephen's dismissive remarks on the evidence provided by the expert witnesses. The general consensus of public opinion was that there had been a miscarriage of justice, with endless columns of newsprint dedicated to the case, and petitions organised throughout the land, including one instigated by the Cleaver brothers in Liverpool, totalling over fifty thousand signatures, whilst in Birmingham a similar public petition totalled over forty thousand. Wagonloads of flowers arrived at Walton Gaol, whilst, in the Houses of Parliament, the Home Secretary had three hefty bundles of petitions dumped on his lap, much to the amusement of the opposition party.

On Wednesday 14th August, Thomas Maybrick, at home in Manchester, opened the morning edition of his local newspaper, and on turning to the correspondence page realised that his brother Michael was in serious trouble.

To the Editor.
There remain a few circumstances in this case that have had a very little airing, and which at least admit of some notice from those who have a penchant for reflection, and the solution of conundrums.
    1. Who had a great antipathy to Mrs. Maybrick?
    2. Who had as much or more access to Mr. Maybrick about the period of his violent attacks than anybody else?
    3. Who had as much chance as anyone else of adding extra 'condiments' to Mr. Maybrick's food or medicine?
    4. Who, on one occasion, administered a pill to Mr. Maybrick causing him illness?
    5. Who made a mistake in stating the pill administered was 'written upon' by a doctor?
    6. Who administered a pill that was not written upon by a doctor to Mr. Maybrick, which pill cause illness?
    7. Who takes charge of the bulk of the deceased's property?

Query: Why is Mrs. Maybrick charged with murder any more than he whose name forms an answer to all the above questions?

Yours
R.F. Muckley, Hope Road, Sale.
Manchester Courier. 15 August 1889.

Michael Maybrick was rightly concerned. The Muckley letter had appeared only a week after Florence's sentencing. Was the article a reflection of public opinion? How many others were already of a similar mind? Rembrandt Fairfax Muckley was a twenty-nine year old commercial traveller, Honorary Captain of the 3rd Battalion Lancashire Fusiliers, whose daringly controversial remarks would undoubtedly have been viewed very seriously by the readers of this widely circulated Lancashire newspaper. The suspect was not named, but nonetheless Michael impulsively, and misguidedly, indicated his intention to instruct lawyers to commence legal proceedings, resulting in the Liverpool Courier raising the stakes by naming him as the subject of the Muckley letter.

LIBEL ACTION BY MR. MICHAEL MAYBRICK
Mr. Michael Maybrick intends to instruct his solicitors to bring an action for libel against the Manchester Courier by reason of its publishing a communication intimating that he had something to do with administering poison. His name is not mentioned in the article, but he is indicated pretty plainly. He is very indignant over the matter.
Liverpool Courier. 27 August 1889.

Almost a fortnight after the article appeared, the following notice was published in yet another popular Lancashire newspaper, offering an apology, whilst once again lifting the veil of anonymity by openly naming Michael Maybrick, and creating even more unwanted controversy.

Referring to my letter of the 15th inst. relating to the above case, I have, since writing the same, learned that the

suggestions made therein are not correct, and hereby beg to tender apologies to Messrs. Michael Maybrick and Thomas Maybrick for causing them to be published. Yours R. F. Muckley.
Manchester and Lancashire General Advertiser. 28 August 1889.

As a matter of routine, a copy of every newspaper would arrive every day on the desk of a junior official within the Home Office, where matters of national security would be vetted, and items of interest or concern forwarded to higher levels, if considered appropriate. Just how far would these articles progress within the corridors of power?

Mr. Rembrandt Fairfax Muckley had well and truly kicked the hornets' nest. Rival newspapers competed to fill their gossip columns, and Michael Maybrick could only watch as his integrity was challenged. All involved in the trial were now considered fair game, and next in the firing line would be Alice Yapp.

After three years of faithful service with Mrs. Gibson, Birkdale, Southport, Alice Yapp left about 1887 to live with the Maybricks at Battlecrease House, Aigburth, where she remained until her mistress was placed upon trial for the murder of her husband, through the discovery of the note to Brierley, which, as will never be forgotten, Alice Yapp was sent to post, and which she found an excuse for opening. Where Alice Yapp is now staying is difficult to determine. It was thought that she was with Mrs. Briggs, at Gateacre, there taking charge of the Maybrick children, but this is not so. She is evidently keeping quiet somewhere until the present indignation aroused against her has subsided, and the children are in the custody of a friend of the family at Aigburth. It cannot now be discussed whether the story she told the police, to the Coroner, to the Magistrates, and finally to the judge and jury, is the truth, or whether through motives

of curiosity or something else, she deliberately opened the letter and invented this implausible excuse. But the fact remains that she did open and read the letter, and that reading of the letter occasioned the investigation and subsequent proceedings which have since agitated the public mind, not only in Great Britain, but in America, and wherever throughout the civilised world newspapers are available. That the girl should have turned traitor is a mystery to those who knew her best, for she was, or professed to be, a sincere friend of her mistress, who now, through her actions, lies under sentence of death in Walton Gaol.
Liverpool Courier. 17 August 1889.

The Maybrick Trial had been followed closely on the other side of the Atlantic, and on the day after the article in the Liverpool Courier, Alice Yapp was receiving unfavourable attention in the New York Herald.

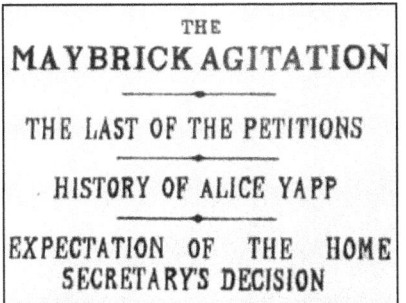

The antecedents of the nurse, Alice Yapp, have been investigated in view of the many assertions which have been made respecting her, and of the extraordinary rumours which have obtained currency as to the condition with the Maybrick poison case.... She managed so to ingratiate herself with the Maybricks, and to obtain such an all-powerful voice in the management of affairs in the servants hall, that she began to do everything possible to get her friends about her .... The tongue of scandal does not leave the name of Alice Yapp alone, and it is said that if further proceedings are taken on the matter, some startling disclosures will be made. New York Herald. 18 August 1889.

In the same newspaper, on the same day, a separate article appeared, posing a series of questions, not dis-similar in intent to those proposed by Mr. R.F. Muckley one week earlier, but this time directed at Alice Yapp.

- *Have you observed the actions of one of the female witnesses have been somewhat remarkable?*
- *Have you observed that it was she that made the first accusations against Mrs. Maybrick; it was she that opened the remarkable letter given to her to post; that it was she that found all, or nearly all, the arsenic; that it was she that started the fly-paper theory; and it was she that set in motion another person, who in their turn set in motion the Maybrick brothers, who in their turn deposed Mrs. Maybrick and made her an object of suspicion?*
- *Did you know anything about this woman?*
- *Do you know whether her devotion to James Maybrick is greater or less than the average devotion of a servant to her master?*
- *Do you know how all that arsenic got into the house?*
- *Has it occurred to you that if any person who knew all the intimate circumstances of Maybrick's way of living desired to cast suspicion on Mrs. Maybrick, it was an easy thing to do?*
- *Do you believe that a woman who desired to poison her husband with arsenic would scatter it in as many directions as the evidence shows it to have been scattered?*

New York Herald. 18 August 1889.

Mr. Muckley's article was mild in comparison. Alice Yapp was not named, but the children's nurse just happened to have been the subject of the earlier exposé in the same newspaper on the same day. The inference was clear, but Alice was in no position to threaten legal action, and Michael Maybrick was certainly not going to become involved. The newshounds were hot on the trail, and no-one was beyond the reach of the press, as proved by the exploits of one particular reporter sent over from New York to publicise the injustice perpetrated on one of its nationals.

A reporter from an American print actually made a desperate attempt to interview the honourable Sir James Fitzjames Stephen on the Maybrick verdict. On Sunday last, the daring reporter in question drove up to Newsham House in a smart turnout, and called to see the judge on important business. The servant, imagining that the visitor was some distinguished gentleman from London, bowed him in, and informed him that his lordship was in his room on the first floor. The stranger, without any more ado, proceeded to mount the stairs, but before he got to the top, the awful figure of the judge himself confronted him, and thereupon the following colloquy is reported to have taken place. 'Well Sir, what do you want?' 'Well, I guess I want to ask your lordship a few questions with reference to this Maybrick affair which you alone can answer.' The judge made a mighty effort to smother his swelling wrath. He succeeded in doing so at last, and then, with a terrible meaning in his words, said, 'There's the door,' and at the same moment turned to the servant, whom he laconically addressed, 'And see he leaves by it.' The would-be interviewer, grasping the situation in a moment, retired discomforted from the scene.
Liverpool Weekly News. 17 August 1889.

If the judge could be so readily targeted, Michael Maybrick must have considered himself equally vulnerable, especially in the wake of the Muckley fiasco. To compound matters, Edwin was becoming a liability, shaken by the public revelation of his dishonesty in tampering with court evidence, and fearful of the consequences of exposure, should their fabrication around the Brierley letter be revealed. Only a few weeks earlier, as the inquest was looming, family friend

Charles Radcliffe had noted, 'Edwin is in bed with nervous prostration. Tom and Michael are seeing to it that he leaves England.' That course of action was never going to happen, but now the Trial was over Michael was able to take Edwin away for a period of recuperation, making a tactical retreat into the obscurity of an isolated cottage on the Isle of Wight.

THE ISLE OF WIGHT

The month of August on the Isle of Wight was idyllic. The Trial was over, Florence Maybrick was destined to meet her fate on the 23rd, and Michael, reflecting on events, had time to gloat over the success of his scheme.

Alice Yapp had lied, Edwin had tampered with evidence, and Michael's complicity in the faked discovery of Florence's suitcase at Battlecrease House had been overlooked. A judge of the calibre of Sir James Fitzjames Stephen would normally have ensured that Alice and Edwin be charged with perjury and contempt of court, but Alice had escaped with a patronising reprimand, with Edwin exonerated from further action at Sir Charles Russell's insistence, before having uttered a word. As for the Brierley letter, not a soul had queried their clever fabrication of events. Michael Maybrick was indeed protected by his guardian angel and spiritual mentor. He was truly invincible. In the words of Florence Aunspaugh,

He had been courted by royalty, the Pope, all the celebrities of the world, and it had turned his head. My father did not like or admire him at all. He said his success had endowed him with a superiority complex, and thought that he had forgotten more than anybody else ever did know ..... he thought he should be classed with Shakespeare, Byron, Milton and Tennyson. My father often laughed and said Michael had already engaged a tomb in Westminster Abbey.
                    Letters of Florence Aunspaugh to Trevor Christie.

Then one morning, Michael and Edwin Maybrick were surprised by a knock on their door. On the doorstep of the cottage stood an American newspaper reporter, inviting comment on a controversial article in the New York Herald, reproduced regionally in newspapers throughout England, in which he had personally interviewed the Baroness von Roques. Michael had no intention of engaging in conversation with the intruder, and was about to send him on his way, but, after a brief exchange, was content to listen as the journalist relayed the contents of the article, which was also printed in the Liverpool Courier.

The following report of an interview with the Baroness von Roques appeared in the London Edition of the New York Herald. 'I am the Baroness von Roques. I am the mother of Mrs. Maybrick, who is my only child. I was very much opposed at first to giving any public statement, but I had and still have full confidence in the courts of England, and hold a conviction that they will not permit a terrible mistake to be made. Mr. Maybrick died on Saturday. Up to the following Friday afternoon my daughter lay ill, prostrate and helpless, without a friend. She was surrounded by enemies, whose bitterness I need not call your attention to, who had prejudiced her in their own minds as a murderess, and who were hotly ransacking her house, a house in which they had no legal right. I met Edwin in the vestibule of the house. He said they had all lost their heads, that Florie was too ill to know anything. He said 'I would never have believed one word against Florie, if it had not been for that letter to Brierley'.

Liverpool Courier. 21 August 1889.

There follows a very important statement by the Baroness, inferring something very suspect about the Brierley letter. Florence was in solitary confinement, unable to pass comment, but the Baroness was determined to express her concerns.

Now permit me to say that there was a great deal of surreptitiousness about the letter to Brierley. It was written

with the knowledge of a woman who had already come to the conclusion, honestly, or dishonestly, that my daughter was a murderess at heart. It was given to that woman to post, and that woman opened it. I may be Mrs. Maybrick's mother, but it looks to me as if that strange and very unnecessary letter, a letter so queerly and ingeniously compromising, that no other possible combination of words could have been equally harmful, was simply a trap, successfully laid and triumphantly executed. My daughter is not a woman of very much penetration. If you could see her you would not wonder at the ease with which she has been deceived.'
Liverpool Courier. 21 August 1889.

Well said, Baroness. A trap, successfully laid, triumphantly executed, and definitely part of a plot. Something didn't quite add up, but the Baroness just couldn't fathom it out. Michael Maybrick listened with concealed horror, as the journalist continued,

.... I believe that those two women, ignorant of all the private circumstances, ignorant of Mr. Maybrick's extensive use of arsenic, came to the conclusion that my daughter was poisoning him. The idea is simply absurd that you can poison a man who has been using arsenic for eleven years, without his knowing or suspecting it. Mr. Maybrick knew his own constitution perfectly well. He had been experimenting on it with drugs ever since I knew him. He, who knew ten times as much about himself and about arsenic as either of these two women, had no suspicion whatever of his wife, while they were bursting with suspicion.
Liverpool Courier. 21 August 1889.

Florence's mother was determined to put the record straight, and to present the facts to a receptive American public, taking care not to cross that delicate line leading to possible legal action. 'These two women' would suffice, as those familiar with the case could fill in the blanks. However, by now the

Baroness was in full flow, and initial caution was about to be cast to the wind. Publish and be damned.

Mrs. Briggs was a very intimate friend of Mr. Maybrick. He had known her long before he met my daughter. He permitted her to visit the house most freely. Mr. Maybrick was an intimate friend of her father, Mr. Janion, and had been on close terms with the Janion family all his life. Mrs. Briggs, from the outset, was a potent factor in the household. She kept a general eye on affairs. Mrs. Briggs had unmarried sisters, and I have no doubt that the opinion prevailed that if Mr. Maybrick's taste had been all that it might to have been, he would have married a Miss Janion. Miss Gertrude Janion, her sister, had been known for a long time in their circle to have been smitten with Mr. Brierley, I am not dealing in trifling gossip in this matter, I am showing you states of mind and motives which bear directly on this case. The pill-box containing Mr. Maybrick's private store of arsenic only turned up at the Trial. It had been kept back. Who knows what else has been kept back? Does the judge know? Do the jury know? Where are Mr. Maybrick's clothes? Have they been examined for arsenic? Have the pockets been examined?

Liverpool Courier. 21 August 1889.

Baroness Caroline Holbrook von Roques would have equalled Sir Charles Russell as defence attorney. Michael Maybrick's peaceful sunny morning in the Isle of Wight countryside had been shattered, but worse was yet to come. The Baroness had not yet finished, and next in the firing line would be Michael Maybrick, who by now had the reporter's full attention.

I would like to know by what right or law the furniture and all the belongings of the house were sold, before the will was proved. I would like to know if, in this part of England, Miss Yapp, Mrs. Briggs and the Maybrick brothers are acting magistrates or not? On the day following Mr. Maybrick's death, Mrs. Briggs and Mrs. Hughes ransacked the house. I would like to know whose right it was to do this work? I went to Michael Maybrick with it. I asked him if it was brotherly or manly? He said he was looking for Mr. Maybrick's keys. He said he wanted the keys to the silver chest to lock up the silver. He said he was afraid of the servants. I said that if the servants had been trusted for four years, they could be trusted still. I asked him why, if he was seeking the keys, he did not look for them himself, instead of committing the search to two women? He made no answer. He said that he never dreamed that there was any question of poison, until the meat juice was analysed. He said 'I should never have thought of poison if Mrs. Briggs had not told me'.

> **THE ATTACK ON MRS. BRIGGS.**
> **IMPENDING ACTION FOR LIBEL.**
>
> We are informed that proceedings for libel will at once be instituted against the *New York Herald* (London edition) for certain alleged libellous allegations made against the character of Mrs. Briggs in its report of an interview with the Baroness von Roque which appeared on Wednesday last.

Liverpool Courier. 21 August 1889.

All four had now been named, Michael Maybrick, Alice Yapp, Martha Hughes and Matilda Briggs, the latter of whom threatened to instigate legal proceedings, but never quite got round to doing so. It had soon become evident in the course of conversation that the reporter was the New York Herald's 'man on the spot', who had not only persuaded the Baroness to grant an interview, but had braved the indignation of His Honour Judge James Fitzjames Stephen by intruding into the Judge's private residence. Now here he was, face to face with

Michael Maybrick, in the front room of his isolated country retreat. Michael felt strangely vulnerable, and after having initially refused to co-operate with the reporter, weighed up the alternatives, soon deciding he had little choice but to comment on the article.

'No one is waiting more anxiously the decision of the Home Secretary relative to Mrs. Maybrick than are Mr. Michael Maybrick and Mr. Edwin Maybrick, brothers of the man for whose death she stands condemned to hang. They are living in a pretty little cottage on the outskirts of the village of St. Helens, Isle of Wight, where they went immediately upon the conclusion of the Trial in Liverpool. 'Nothing would please me more now,' said Michael Maybrick, when called upon by a representative of the New York Herald, 'than to hear that the Home Secretary's decision is that Mrs. Maybrick shall go free.' Mr. Maybrick declined at first to be interviewed, but on being told that reports had been sent from Liverpool reflecting severely upon him, he changed his mind, and talked freely, 'What are the reports?' he asked. Being told that one was that he had known Alice Yapp before she entered her brother's household, and that he had put her there to be a spy upon Mrs. Maybrick, he replied, 'I never knew or heard of her until long after she was engaged there, and I do not think I spoke a word to her until I was summoned to my brother's bedside shortly before he died. Why would I want to have a spy on Mrs. Maybrick, I should like to know? My relations with her were always pleasant. She has come to me time and again for money and one thing and another, and she always got it. Only three weeks before my brother died, the day after she was with Brierley, in fact, I took her to dine at the Café Royal, in Regent Street, and took her to the theatre. Does that look as if I disliked and distrusted her? I never but once spoke harshly to her, and that was when I told her I had grave suspicions of poisoning in my brother's case. I have no enmity of poisoning in my brother's case, I have no enmity

against her, and do not want to be understood as making any charge against her.'

'Did you see nothing in the actions or manner of Mrs. Briggs or Miss Yapp that suggested to you that they might be hostile to Mrs. Maybrick?' 'No. I did not. Mrs. Briggs came to the house only when she was invited to come. Miss Yapp seemed to be a straightforward, honest sort of woman.' 'Do you not think that your brother used arsenic?' 'No, I do not. If he had used it, I would have been certain to know of it. I never saw the slightest indication of his using arsenic. He was not a man to use poison. The chemist, Heaton, who said he sold him pick-me-ups, was simply mistaken in the man.' 'What have you to say regarding the statement of the Baroness von Roques, published in the Herald?' 'I have no desire to say anything against the Baroness, but many of her statements are untrue, and her story as a whole is misleading .... I was not gruff at all, nor disposed to be. She says in effect that I tried to cover the search of the house for arsenic, by saying I was looking for the keys, so I could lock up the silver. Nothing of the kind happened. I never mentioned the word 'keys' and had absolutely nothing to do with the search. The police did that. The incident was purely an invention.' Mr. Edwin Maybrick was present during the interview, and corroborated many of the words uttered by his brother.

Evening Express. 21 August 1889.

A tacit agreement appears to have been reached with the reporter not to involve Edwin, from whom the occasional silent nod within the interview would be taken as corroboration of Michael's remarks. Delighted with his scoop, the intrepid reporter made off in haste, and the article appeared in print that very evening. Michael Maybrick had made his views known in such an assertive manner, with his denial of involvement in the search expressed with such vehemence, that he was convinced his statement would be read as true. How unfortunate that Mr. Thomas Addison, in his opening address on behalf of the Crown, a few weeks earlier, seemed to differ, supported by testaments from Edwin and Mrs. Briggs at the earlier hearings.

'Now directly he was dead, Michael Maybrick directed Alice Yapp and Bessie Brierley, the housemaid, to look and see what they could find.'

Thomas Addison. Crown Court.

'On Sunday, the 12th May, I, Michael and Mrs. Briggs searched the dressing room of the deceased's bedroom.

Edwin Maybrick.

'On the following day, I searched some of the rooms, Mr. Michael and Mr. Edwin Maybrick being with me at the time.'

Mrs. Briggs. Magistrates Court.

Michael Maybrick, accustomed to dominating conversations with bombastic and dismissive rhetoric, would soon come to realise that on this occasion no amount of pomposity would alter the fact that his every word was on record. Hot bluster did not translate well into cold print, and he would now be held accountable in the national press, leaving readers to ponder over Michael Maybrick's credibility as leading witness for the prosecution. Press coverage of the Maybrick Trial was now unprecedented, all involved were vulnerable to close scrutiny, and powerful figures within the Establishment were following reports and public opinion very closely indeed.

TOM MERRY

Michael Maybrick was in deeply pensive mood. Those press reports were extremely disconcerting, with repercussions from the trial affecting not only himself, but the acolytes he had somehow managed to implicate in his private vendetta. The last thing he needed was the nation's favourite satirical cartoonist on his case but, as fate would have it, the Maybrick Trial had caught the attention of Tom Merry, whose mischievously perceptive weekly press contributions to the St. Stephen's Review were immensely popular at the time.

Prime Ministers Gladstone and Salisbury had been the subject of Merry's pictorial lampooning, and now would be the turn of Henry Matthews, stewing over the fate of Florence Maybrick. This cartoon, published on the 17th August, 1889, portrays the Home Secretary sitting in judgement between Florence Maybrick and Jack the Ripper, bearing a placard,

'Hang the Wanton. Murder Her.' Beneath the cartoon was the caption, 'Whitechapel at Whitehall. Attempted murder of Florence Maybrick. Save her Mr. Matthews.' The inference is staggering. What on earth did Jack the Ripper, evidently still very much alive, have to do with the Maybrick case, and why would the Whitechapel Murderer want Florence Maybrick dead? Michael Maybrick, seeing himself mirrored in the cartoon, knew the answer, but so now did someone else. What or who had motivated the artist to conjure up such an image, and what would the public make of it?

Bro. William Mecham, pen-name Tom Merry, had been initiated two years earlier into Kennington Lodge No.1381, at once expanding his circle of political acquaintances, some of whom would have relished the opportunity of leaking, in the strictest confidence, salacious gossip which could conveniently make or break a career by inclusion in a single cartoon. The current talk of the town was the Maybrick Trial, over which the tide of public opinion had well and truly turned in favour of Florence Maybrick, now a 'cause celebre', and the subject of national campaigns and rallies, championed by Alexander MacDougall, courting controversy, provoking public concern, and avidly seeking press coverage.

One week prior to the publication of the cartoon, the first 'Free Florence' meeting in London had been convened by Mr. MacDougall at the Cannon Street Hotel, where the ambitious young artist may well have seized the opportunity to engage the old firebrand barrister in conversation over a drink or two. 'Where's there's smoke there's fire,' was the driving force behind political satire, and Alexander MacDougall had plenty of both to offer the receptive listener.

The resultant cartoon not only affirms Tom Merry's belief in the content, but may be the first indication that not only did someone suspect Michael Maybrick of murdering his own brother, but a further eight women on the streets of Whitechapel. Michael Maybrick's weapon of choice, suspicion, had come back to haunt him.

Tom Merry was sitting on the scoop of a lifetime, but his alter ego, Bro. William Mecham, was bound by a solemn oath to uphold the principles of fraternal Masonic loyalty, and to say nothing. Bro. Michael Maybrick was an acting Grand Officer, attending Grand Lodge meetings in the personal company of HRH. Bro. the Prince of Wales, and it would not have been long before someone in high office offered a quiet word of advice to Tom Merry that he drop the subject. No further Maybrick based cartoons appeared, and Tom Merry would maintain his vow of silence, although on rare occasions, in later life, may have let slip his belief of possible Masonic and Royal connections. Mere rumours, of course, mere rumours. Within the corridors of power, discussions were taking place, and meetings were convened in the Home Office as a matter of urgency, with Judge Stephen summoned on the 16th and 21st August to respond to representations submitted by the defence, and to consider possible grounds for reprieve, without impugning his own integrity. Powerful figures within the Establishment, however, were very much against such a course of action, and the Home Secretary found himself in a very difficult position when Sir Godfrey Lushington, Permanent Under-Secretary to the Home Office, very influential in diplomatic circles, made his official view quite clear in a private letter to Sir Henry Matthews.

This is a case where there should be no interference with the sentence, unless the verdict of the jury is the subject of reasonable doubt. Having read the papers with careful attention, I have no doubt whatsoever that the verdict was right. I am completely satisfied that Mr. Maybrick died of arsenic, and that the prisoner administered arsenic.

> THE
> # MAYBRICK VERDICT
>
> NO WORD FROM THE HOME SECRETARY.
>
> Home Secretary and Justice Stephen Threatened.
>
> PREPARING FOR THE EXECUTION.
>
> Erecting the Scaffold at Walton.

Sir Godfrey Lushington.
20th August 1889.
HO1441638/50678.

Judge Stephen's middle son was Henry Lushington Stephen. His youngest was James Kenneth Stephen, tutor to Prince Albert Victor, eldest son of HRH Edward, Prince of Wales, the future King of England. Judge James Fitzjames Stephen was at the very heart of the British Establishment.

Henry Matthews was not one to be swayed by public opinion, nor by Sir Godfrey Lushington. Medical experts were called in to expound on matters requiring further clarification, events at Battlecrease House were re-examined, and, intriguingly, the original Blucher letter, in its entirety, was demanded for perusal, which must have involved a direct approach to Michael Maybrick. Even more intriguingly, handwritten on the accompanying cover note to the Blucher letter, filed in Home Office records, are the words 'Mr. Matthews, Mr. Maybrick's letter in no way implies his belief that he was being poisoned by his wife', a strong indication that the letter was under serious investigation. Mr. Matthews had much to consider. On the 23rd August, only three days before Florence was due to hang by the neck until dead, the Home Office issued the following statement,

We are given to understand that the Home Secretary, after fullest consideration, and after taking the best legal and medical advice that could be obtained, has advised her Majesty to respite the capital punishment of Florence Elizabeth Maybrick, and to commute the punishment to penal servitude for life; inasmuch as, although the evidence leads to the conclusion that the prisoner administered and attempted to administer arsenic to her husband with intent to murder him, yet it does not wholly exclude a reasonable doubt whether his death was in fact caused by the administration of arsenic. The decision is understood not to imply the slightest reflection on the able and experienced practitioners who gave evidence, or on the tribunal before which the prisoner was tried. We understand that the course adopted has the concurrence of the learned judge.

HO/144/1639/A50678.

Henry Matthews had produced a judgement conceding reasonable doubt on the verdict, but not on the judicial process. Had reasonable doubt been accepted by the court, Florence Maybrick would have walked free, yet here we have the Home Secretary conceding reasonable doubt, but imposing a life sentence for an offence with which the prisoner had never been charged or tried, that of attempted murder. Florence Maybrick could not legally be sentenced for such an offence, yet that is precisely what the Home

Secretary had done. Unsurprisingly, whilst concurring with the life saving reprieve, the judiciary was soon up in arms at such an outrageous irregularity, but her Majesty had given her seal of approval to the recommendation, as a consequence of which the Home Secretary's decision was final and binding. Arrangements were made for Florence to be transferred to Woking Female Convict Prison, held initially in solitary confinement, clothed in arrow insignia prison tunic, and forbidden to speak without permission, in a cell measuring eight feet by five, with hammock, table, chair and bucket. Restricted visits were eventually permitted, lasting thirty minutes, with visitors separated from the prisoner by two metal grills in between of which was seated a female warder. Conversation was strictly vetted, and failure to confirm would result in forfeiture of further visits. Once a year, photographs of three close relatives were permitted, which, for the initial year of confinement, had to be returned within twenty four hours. This sad privilege was evidently too compassionate for Michael Maybrick, still intent on vengeance.

The innocents, my children, are a baby of three years, the other a boy of seven, all I had left behind in the world. During the early years of my imprisonment I received my children's photographs once a year, also several friendly letters from Mr. Thomas Maybrick, with information about them. But, as time passed on, these ceased altogether. When I could endure the silence no longer, I instructed Mr. R.S. Cleaver of Liverpool, who had been my solicitor in my case, to write to Mr. Michael Maybrick to forward fresh photographs of my boy and girl. To this request Mr. Thomas Maybrick replied that Mr. Michael Maybrick refused to permit.

Mrs. Maybrick's Own Story. Florence Maybrick.

> **A VISIT TO WOKING CONVICT PRISON.**
>
> **MRS. MAYBRICK AND OTHER FEMALE PRISONERS.**
>
> A correspondent, giving an account of the recent visit to Woking Female Convict Prison, says the building is in the midst of the prettiest part of Surrey; and although providing accommodation for 720 convicts, has at present only 310. Madame Rachel, notorious as a beautifier, and Constance Kent, connected with the Road murder, were confined here; but the best-known prisoners now confined there are Mrs. Gordon Baillie, the noted swindler, and Mrs. Maybrick. For life prisoners there is no fixed rule, their cases being considered by the Home Office periodically or upon petition. Mrs. Gordon-Baillie and Mrs. Maybrick are entirely different in style and physique, but prison dress and the method of wearing the hair is a great leveller as to appearance. Both prisoners are in excellent health. Mrs. Maybrick is in the probation class, which undergoes solitary confinement for the first nine months. This class wears a red star on the arm, which denotes that the wearers have not before been convicted of serious crime, though some of them, like Mrs. Maybrick, had been tried on the capital charge. The Home Office authorities have taken exception to many statements lately made in reference to Woking. It was announced that since the arrival of Mrs. Maybrick the prison chapel had been crowded each Sunday. As a matter of fact, the chapel is not open to the public, the only visitors allowed being the relatives of officers or friends residing with them, and then only with the governor's sanction. On the first Sunday after Mrs. Maybrick's arrival at the prison there were no visitors, and on the second Sunday the number was but three.
>
> It is believed that the Emperor William will visit Constantinople after leaving Athens.

Florence's silence was crucial, and, if unclaimed by prison fever, she would have to live with the torment of just how much control Michael Maybrick exercised over her. The children would be held hostage. On the 30th September, Baroness Von Roques wrote to the Liverpool Echo.

The following letter from Mrs. Maybrick's mother has been received by a Liverpool friend.

'I am grieved at the unexpected conduct of the Maybrick brothers regarding my daughter's dear little children. I have heard from the solicitors that they decline to furnish any information as to the whereabouts of the children. My unhappy daughter in her last letter from Walton stated that she desired Dr. Hopper and the solicitors to have access to them at stated intervals, and, if possible, they were to be with me. Who has a greater right to protect them than I, their grandmother? Surely *the ties of maternity and of blood ought to be respected. The intentions of the Messrs. Maybrick, if honest and true, need not be shrouded in such mystery. Do they belong to the Maybrick brothers more than my daughter, or to me? The anxious thoughts and doubts about these poor darling children have caused my daughter greater pain than anything else in the dreadful ordeal she has gone through. Her heart is breaking for some scrap of information about them.* '

Liverpool Echo. 30 September 1889.

Florence Maybrick was locked alone in her cell, racked with grief and anguish, and it would have been little consolation to learn, two years after her conviction, that Judge James Fitzjames Stephen was considered unfit for office.

Though Sir James Fitzjames Stephen was able, in some fashion, to resume his duties, his mental capacity soon became the subject of general comment. Even the press could not keep silent, but the one man who could not see that his intellect had failed was Sir J.F. Stephen himself. At last the clamour became too loud. He was induced to consult an eminent physician, who insisted on his early retirement. This took place in 1891. Sir J.F. Stephen lived for three years longer, but seems never to be able to write or speak in public again. He died, I believe, in a private lunatic asylum.

J.H. Levy. The Necessity for Criminal Appeal.

The legal fraternity realised in no time at all that something very remiss was happening at the Home Office, again best summed up by lawyer J.H. Levy, in his authoritative book 'The Necessity for Criminal Appeal, as Illustrated by the Maybrick Case'.

> THE
> # NECESSITY FOR CRIMINAL APPEAL
> AS ILLUSTRATED BY
> ## THE MAYBRICK CASE
> AND THE
> JURISPRUDENCE OF VARIOUS COUNTRIES.
>
> EDITED BY
> J H LEVY

It is well known that the Lord Chief Justice of England, and the Recorder of Liverpool, who were both present at the Trial, are strongly of the opinion that Mrs. Maybrick ought not to have been convicted. This is enough, in itself, to create a doubt in the minds of most reasonable people. But quite apart from such probabilities, this case is, in my opinion, one of the most extraordinary miscarriages of justice of modern times. When it is realised by the British public that Mrs. Maybrick has been doomed to life-long imprisonment on the strength of a secret dossier, for a crime for which she was never been publicly tried, the result will be a revulsion as has not been experienced in England for many a long day.

J.H. Levy.

Secret dossier? J.H. Levy was an authority on the Maybrick Trial and subsequent repercussions, which would result in the introduction of the Criminal Appeal Act, 1907, establishing a right of appeal so sadly lacking hitherto. Levy was not given to choosing his words lightly, so reference to a secret dossier would have been made only after careful deliberation. To fully appreciate the ramifications of the Home Office's abject refusal to grant justice for Florence Maybrick, events six years later are worthy of consideration.

In 1895, six years after Sir Henry Matthews' announcement of a reprieve, Sir Charles Russell had been appointed Lord Chief Justice of England, and was still vigorously campaigning on Florence's behalf, but without success, despite his position at the pinnacle of the judicial system. After a hotly contested election that summer, the Tory party had succeeded in ousting the Liberals from power, and with them went Sir Henry Matthews, to be replaced as Home Secretary in June of that year by Sir Matthew White Ridley, On the 22nd August, the anniversary of Florence's reprieve from the death sentence, Mr. T.P. O'Connor stood in the Houses of Parliament, and addressed the new Home Secretary.

Mr. T.P. O'Connor (Liverpool, Scotland), said he quite appreciated the danger in the public interest of making the House of Commons a Court of Appeal in Criminal Cases, and a member was only justified in bringing to the notice of the House of Commons a case of very great urgency and importance. The judge who tried the case was now dead, and he believed the conviction of the woman was largely due to reflections on the evidence by the judge. It was proved that the woman had been untrue to her marriage vows. The judge, in his address to the jury, laid an enormous amount of stress on that office, which was not the offence with which she was charged, and the feeling was created that, as she had been found guilty of adultery, she must therefore be found guilty of murder. The Home Secretary declared that it was not proved that Mr. Maybrick had died of poison administered by Mrs. Maybrick. Therefore, Mrs. Maybrick was not guilty of murder, and was either entitled to a new trial, or to be set free. He therefore asked the Home Secretary to consult the Lord Chief Justice on the case, and he trusted the Rt. Hon. Gentleman's view on the case would result in his being able to pass a more favourable judgement upon it than his predecessors in the Office had been able to.

Hansard. 22 August. Vol. 36. cc 581- 652.

Sir Godfrey Lushington had retired as Permanent under Secretary at the same time as the outgoing Home Secretary, but the Earl of Lathom was still Lord Chamberlain, and would remain so for three more years under the new Prime Minister, Lord Salisbury, occupying that office for the second time. Bro. the Earl of Lathom was Provincial Grand Master of Lancashire, whilst the new Home Secretary, Bro. Sir Matthew White Ridley, was Provincial Grand Master of Northumberland, both powerful figures within Freemasonry. In no time at all, the incoming Home Secretary would have been entrusted with the closely guarded secret shared only by a select band of men within the Establishment, that Florence Maybrick either knew, or had good reason to have suspected, the identity of the Whitechapel Murderer. The new Home Secretary duly responded to the question proposed by the Honourable Member for Liverpool.

Sir, M. White Ridley, Secretary of State for the Home Dept., said that it was impossible for a man in his position to deal with all the arguments that were necessarily brought to bear on them, publicly, arguments that were necessarily brought to bear on them publicly, but it must be notorious to gentlemen of any experience or knowledge of criminal matters that there was a very great deal, not of absolute evidence, but a great deal of private information, which was impossible for anybody occupying his position to make public. Hansard. 22 August. Vol 36. cc581-652

> **THE MAYBRICK CASE DRAMATISED.**
>
> **SEVERE LETTER FROM THE STAGE CENSOR.**
>
> At the monthly meeting of the Wigan Town Council, held yesterday, applications were received from the lessees of the Royal Court Theatre and the Theatre Royal asking for licences for the performance of stage plays under the new Local Government Act. In the case of the first-named theatre the licence was granted for a month.
>
> It was proposed that a similar course be taken with the Theatre Royal, but after the reading of a letter from Mr. E. F. S. Pigott, dated from the Lord Chamberlain's office, an amendment was proposed that the licence be not granted. The letter, which had been in the first case forwarded to Mr. Fred Lichfield, a late lessee of the theatre, and had been returned through the Dead Letter Office, was then forwarded to the Town-clerk of Wigan. It reads as follows:—
>
> Sir,—The Lord Chamberlain is informed that the Theatre Royal, Wigan, under your management as licensee, on Friday evening, the 6th September ult., a new stage play which had not been submitted for examination and licence, as the law requires, was performed, entitled, "Florence Maybrick; or, Is She Guilty?" described as the playbill of the theatre as embracing "the principal incidents in the late Maybrick case." The representation of an unlicensed play is a distinct and wilful violation of the law, but the production of such a piece as this, which could never have been sanctioned by the licensers of stage plays, is moreover an outrage on public decency, a flagrant insult to the administration of justice in this country, and calculated to bring the law in contempt. Such performances are a disgrace and a degradation to the art and profession of the stage, and must be repudiated with disgust by every respectable manager and member of the profession. A copy of the enclosed circular to provincial managers was forwarded to you some time since, but whether you received it or not, it is assumed that the managers of respectable theatres have made themselves acquainted with the provisions of the law and the regulations of this department, with which they are immediately concerned. Had this scandalous performance been notified to the Lord Chamberlain beforehand, it would have been my duty to bring it to the notice of the local licensing authorities, with a view to their taking such action as might seem fit on the next licensing day. I am, sir, your obedient servant,
>
> EDWARD F. S. PIGOTT.

So, officially recorded in Hansard, is an open admission that within the portals of the Establishment was a dossier of private information on the Maybrick case, which could not possibly be revealed to the general public. So intent was the Lord Chamberlain on suppressing Florence's cause that on the 6th September 1895, he personally instigated the inept suppression of a parochial theatrical presentation being held in Wigan, only six miles away from the Earl's fiefdom of Latham. This inoffensive and light-hearted production, 'Florence Maybrick. Is She Guilty?', was a satirical reflection on the miscarriage of justice in the Maybrick case, very possibly pursuant to the controversial Tom Merry cartoon.

The play was ironically branded by the Earl of Lathom, a 'distinct and wilful violation of the law, an outrage on public decency, and a flagrant insult to the administration of justice in this country.' Fine words from a man intent on depriving an innocent woman of her freedom.

The main grounds of the continued imprisonment of this most unhappy woman are as mysterious as they ever were. We should at all events now know the charge and the evidence, and the British public would be relieved from the thought that a woman, whom some of the most eminent judges believe to have been wrongly condemned, is suffering a living death in a British prison, on the strength of a secret dossier.

J.H. Levy.

At the time of the Trial, in August of 1889, a self-appointed and self-serving priesthood, at the highest level of the British Establishment, believed that Florence knew the identity of the Whitechapel Murderer, and as a consequence, had to be silenced one way or another. Michael Maybrick had so far ensured that James remained their main suspect, but recent press articles were showing Michael in a suspicious light, his integrity was in question, and his murder of Alice Mackenzie had been a gross miscalculation. Alexander MacDougall was becoming increasing inquisitive, assertive to the point of near accuracy, and Michael Maybrick was now more vulnerable than at any time on the streets of Whitechapel. The funny little games were well and truly over, to be replaced by a potentially serious situation.

'Do not shirk this question. Let every single one of my readers answer it, and recollect that this woman is now passing a living death in our midst and, recollecting this, insist upon an answer to it, insist upon knowing whether it was James Maybrick's symptoms or Michael Maybrick's suggestions, which led these two doctors, Dr. Humphreys and Dr. Carter, on that Thursday, to come to the conclusion that

James Maybrick was suffering from irritant poisoning, most possibly arsenic.'
Alexander MacDougall. The Maybrick Case.

The cottage on the Isle of Wight had offered peace and tranquillity, and whilst Michael Maybrick was quite capable of maintaining a calm composure, his mind was now in turmoil, and Edwin's mental state could prove problematical. Should steps be taken to fabricate more substantive evidence to incriminate James if the need were to arise? Just in case?

MR. MILLER

On the 16th September, the following article appeared in 'The Mirror', a small circulation illustrated newspaper, whose editor, Stuart Cumberland, had been following the Whitechapel Murders in his columns over the previous few weeks.

'A gentleman is making the rounds of the publishers with what he claims to be the diary of Mrs. Maybrick. The diary, he says, was found in a trunk after the conviction of Mrs. Maybrick, and it purports to contain impressions and confessions from early childhood up to the present year. If the diary is to be believed, the 'unhappy lady' now languishing in Woking Gaol, must have been of an extremely skittish disposition. We are not exactly convinced of the genuineness of the documents, although as far as we can glean, the genuineness of them is guaranteed. The object of those into whose hands the alleged diary has fallen appears to be to publish a 'shilling shocker.'
The Mirror. 16 September 1889.

A 'shilling shocker' was a short story magazine of sensational content, a fairly apt encapsulation of Michael's intentions. Within hours, the story was picked up by a reporter from the Liverpool Echo.

'Mr. Stuart Cumberland, questioned as to the statement in his paper about Mrs. Maybrick's diary having been offered for sale to a London publisher, said that he expected the diary would come into his own hands: if it did he would certainly publish it if he thought it to be authentic, and if he did not, he would denounce the imposter who was endeavouring to palm it off as authentic. The diary, which was in three small volumes, tied together with a blue silken cord, was taken by a gentleman who declined to give his name to Messrs. Triscler & Co. the Ludgate Circus publisher. He said that he was a

member of the Maybrick family, and had found the books in a box of Mrs. Maybrick's at Battlecrease House.'

Liverpool Echo. 16 September 1889.

Which gentleman relative of the Maybrick family had access to a box in Battlecrease House owned by Florence Maybrick? Even if the diary had not been found during the original searches, there was ample opportunity for further probing when Michael and Edwin had supervised the house clearance on the 25th May.

'The gentleman was seen by the manager of the firm, who himself examined the diary, and expressed his belief in its authenticity. He said that the writing in each of the three books is different, although it is of the same writer. The first book contains Mrs. Maybrick's childhood reminiscences, the second, those of her girlhood, and the third, her married life. The manager was unable to decide what offer to make in the absence of the head of the firm, so he told the gentleman to call again, at the same time advising him that it might be worth his while to offer the books to Mr. Stuart Cumberland, who would, no doubt, be glad to speculate upon them, or to the Baroness von Roques, who might possibly purchase them to prevent their publication.'

Liverpool Echo. 16 September 1889.

Why would the Baroness be anxious to prevent publication? Did the diaries contain intimate details of the Brierley affair, or perhaps salacious references to Florence's life before meeting James? It is no coincidence that this episode took place during the Maybrick brothers' period of reflection and reassessment on the Isle of Wight, when all options to discredit Florence were under consideration.

With the very real prospect of being identified in London, Michael would have had no intention of direct involvement in this venture, so Edwin had been delegated the task, and dispatched from the Isle of Wight to London. Deeply unhappy at the situation in which he found himself, and on edge from the outset of this meeting, mention of reference to the indomitable Baroness would have really concentrated Edwin's mind. What was he letting himself in for? Without further ado, after this close encounter, Edwin had evidently beaten a hasty retreat, never to return.

'Nothing has since been heard of the diary, so it is probable that the latter suggestion was the one adopted, and that the Baroness von Roques now possesses the unhappy daughter's diary, which therefore will never see the light of day.'

Liverpool Echo. 16 September 1889.

The Baroness von Roques was the very last person Edwin wished to encounter, with his nervous disposition already shaken by Stuart Cumberland's earlier threat to denounce any imposters involved in the diary's provenance. Michael, as usual, had opted to remain in the shadows whilst Edwin did as he was told, and it should have come as no surprise when his brother re-appeared at the Isle of White cottage, diary in hand, vowing to have no further involvement in this hare-brained scheme. The sale had been intended to be swift and anonymous, maximum impact with minimum input, but such had not turned out to be the case, and two weeks later Stuart Cumberland was still pursuing the matter.

'The alleged 'Maybrick Diary' to which reference was made in the Mirror a fortnight ago, is still, I understand, in the hands of those who claim to have discovered it. I am not yet satisfied as to its genuineness, but those who have examined

it appear to be convinced that it is all that it is represented to be. Will Mr. Miller, the gentleman who owns the manuscript, call or communicate with me at the Mirror Office.'.
The Mirror. 30 September 1889.

So the anonymous gentleman was a 'Mr. Miller'. On the same day the following article appeared in the Liverpool Echo.

The following letter from Mrs. Maybrick's mother has been received by a Liverpool friend. 'A statement was circulated in London recently that three volumes of my daughter's diary had been taken from one of the boxes at Battlecrease House by a relative of the family, and offered for sale, and that I had given a large price for them in order to suppress them. There is no truth whatever in this statement. My daughter did not keep a diary. It is quite true that some books are missing; it is supposed that they have been taken away by someone interested in my daughter's downfall. We have wanted these books since my arrival in England after my daughter's arrest. It is always a matter of regret that my daughter's papers and effects, as well as all the household effects, were disposed of with such undue haste after the Trial.'
Liverpool Echo. 30 September 1889.

Michael would have taken great delight in anointing Edwin with the pseudonym 'Mr. Miller.' Apart from the obvious connection with Miller's Court, where Florence's alter-ego Mary Jane Kelly had met her end, half of the letters in 'Miller' just happen to be found in 'Maybrick', and, as with 'M. Baynard', there is a literary significance. In Geoffrey Chaucer's Canterbury Tales, written in Middle English in the fifteenth century, is to be found the Miller's Tale, telling of an older man with a pretty young wife, who was maintaining secret affairs with two younger men. The following is an updated extract from the medieval text.

'This carpenter had recent wed a wife,
Whom he loved more than his life, She was eighteen years of age, Jealous was he, for she was wild and young, and he was old.
Man should wed to status,
For youth and old age are oft in conflict,
Fair was his wife and therewithal ,
Her body graceful and slender,
And surely she had a wanton eye,
That one day this clever clerk,
With this young wife did flirt and play,
My husband is full of jealousy,
You must be very secret.'

Whilst Michael and Edwin were very much a topic of speculation and controversy, within days it would be the turn of James Maybrick to be subjected to scrutiny in this exposé by William Stead, former editor of the Pall Mall Gazette,

James Maybrick was a seducer, an adulterer, and a debauchee. Before he married a young and innocent girl, he seduced a young woman of eighteen, under promises of marriage. He kept her as his mistress until she bore him five children, then he cast her off without remorse when he saw his chance of marrying poor Florence. After his marriage he continued occasionally to meet his mistress, paying her more or less irregularly, a miserable pittance for her maintenance. But that was not all. James Maybrick was false to the young wife whom he had brought to this polluted home. His relations with loose women could have been proved in court, and as a result of his misconduct, mutual relations were suspended for the last two years of his life. He said that he did not wish to injure any child he might have.

Review of Reviews. October 1892.

Who could have provided such a personal insight into the life of James Maybrick? Another carefully timed leak to the press, this time paving the way for a character assassination of his own brother. Was that last sentence indicative of a venereal disease, and, if so, had this caused James, already a hypochondriac, to become mentally unstable on occasions? Had this been the subject of late night brandy fuelled sessions with Michael over Christmas at Battlecrease House, exploiting a common hatred of whores, and fantasising over retribution, extending to subliminal incitement to murder, an ideal solution to Michael's fixation with eliminating Florence? Was James actually primed for murder by Michael, yet fearful and incapable of enacting the deed? An ideal scenario for presentation of New Year's diary to James, in which to commit his troubled mind to print, release the pressures, exorcise the demons.

Now was the time for Michael Maybrick, in the seclusion of a cottage on the Isle of Wight, to put his contingency plan into operation. Four months earlier, the search for James's personal diary would have been the prime objective in the hunt for James's keys on the day following his death. Sections of that diary would now be incorporated into a brand new ledger, a compilation of James's drink and drug fuelled diary entries and Michael's manic ramblings, a devious fabrication of fact and fantasy, purportedly written in its entirety by James, confessing to the Whitechapel murders and signed 'Jack the Ripper', an insurance policy to be secreted away for production only in the event of suspicion falling directly onto Michael Maybrick, the possibility of which could no longer be dismissed out of hand.

Michael Maybrick opened the trunk in the corner of the room, took out James's diary and his own bundle of scribbled diatribes compiled over the last twelve months, walked over to the table, and poured a large brandy.

OLD FRIENDS

As autumn faded into winter, the prospect of Masonic commitments dictated Michael's presence in London, and in mid-December, together with Edwin, he travelled the eighty miles from the Isle of Wight to Wellington Mansions, Regent's Park, fastidiously maintained in his absence by loyal housekeeper, Laura Withers.

Somewhat surprisingly for a man who preferred his own company, Michael Maybrick had cultivated a small close-knit circle of acquaintances, dating back to the time when he enlisted with the Artists Rifles, and socialised with the Toynbee Hall set, of whom a fair number were of a similar misogynistic disposition. As well as the more renowned members of the Artists Rifles would have been fellow recruits, drilling companions with whom he developed a close camaraderie, one of whom merits special attention. Bernard Alfred Quaritch, junior partner in his father's firm, Bernard Quaritch and Co; Antiquarian Booksellers and Publishers, joined the Artists Rifles in 1885, declared age 18, real age 16, just prior to Michael Maybrick, declared age 40, real age 45, one wishing to appear older, and the other younger. Regardless of their age difference, the two would become lifelong friends.

In the following year, 1886, a new librarian had been appointed at Toynbee Hall, Charles Edward Sayle, a larger than life character, who attracted a following from the young intelligentsia of Cambridge University.

Sayle was one of the patrons of Cambridge's intellectual social life, holding salons in his rooms at 8, Trumpington Street, offering introductions to Cambridge's interlocking

social cliques. Sayle was gay, and termed the young men who congregated at Trumpington Street, his Swans.
Biography of George Mallory. Peter and Leni Gillman.

Charles Sayle's salon, a circle of bright, handsome, and predominantly homosexual young men who congregated at his house in Cambridge, included Rupert Brooke, George Mallory, Augustus Bartholomew, and Geoffrey Keynes. Sayle's publisher was Bernard Quaritch, a bookseller who specialised in unpopular but praiseworthy scholarly publications
Wikipedia.

At the same time as Sayle, Maybrick and Quaritch were integrating into the newly created environment of Toynbee Hall, Prince Albert Victor, 'Prince Eddy,' next in line to the throne after the Prince Regent, was also a regular visitor as head of the Toynbee Association, a position he embraced with enthusiasm. Eddy, 22 years old and intellectually challenged, was under the Cambridge tutorship of James Kenneth Stephen, barrister-at-law, five years older than the Prince, and second son of Sir James Fitzjames Stephen, the controversial judge at the Maybrick Trial. Within the very limited confines of Toynbee Hall, Michael Maybrick and J.K. Stephen may well have become acquaintances, flamboyant characters united by an inherent hatred of women, menacingly latent within the former, and openly flaunted by the latter, displaying a disturbing commonality of views on the elimination of prostitutes in the following composition.

One night, returning from a spree,
With customary whore-lust he
Made up his mind to call and see
The Harlot of Jerusalem.
For although he paid his women well,
This syphilitic spawn of hell,

Struck down each year, and tolled the bell,
For the harlots of Jerusalem.

J.K. Stephen.

He also had an inherent love of his fellow men, a trait shared with former Cambridge resident and newly appointed librarian Charles Sayle, together with a number of acolyte graduates attracted to Toynbee Hall at around the same time.

Prince Eddy, head of the Toynbee Association, soon developed a close bond with J.K. Stephen, which has been the subject of conjecture and controversy to the present day. All indications are that within Toynbee Hall there existed a covert clique of like-minded misogynists, united by a common bond in an age of Victorian suppression, one of whom had cultivated an obsession for retribution against a harlot encountered many years ago, an obsession which would spawn one of the greatest conundrums in criminology. Now, in late 1889, these friends and acquaintances, together with other artistic colleagues sympathetic to Michael Maybrick's decline in popularity, would rally to his support.

> A little while ago some of Mr Michael Maybrick's fellow artists proposed to give him a complimentary concert, marking the occasion of his re-entry into public life after recent events to which no definite allusion need be made. Mr Maybrick deeply appreciated the feeling which prompted the offer, but, on consideration, felt bound to decline it. The *Daily Telegraph* thinks the wisest course has been taken. Mr Maybrick requires no proof of the fact that he has the respect and esteem of the musical public, and a demonstration is, on various grounds, better avoided.

A little while ago, some of Michael Maybrick's fellow artists proposed to give him a complementary concert, marking the occasion of his re-entry into public life, after recent events to which no illusion need be made. Mr. Maybrick deeply appreciated the feeling which promoted this offer, but, on consideration, felt bound to decline it. The Daily Telegraph thinks the wisest course has been taken. Mr. Maybrick requires no proof of the fact that he has the respect and esteem of the musical public, and a demonstration is, on various grounds, better avoided.

South Wales Echo. 16 December 1889.

No better insight could be afforded to illustrate Maybrick's dilemma than the subliminal inferences within that well-meaning article ... *'recent events to which no definite allusion need be made ....the wisest course has been taken'* The concert could have been a public relations disaster. Any moves towards re-assimilation would have to be gradual, if indeed it would ever happen. Not so, however, the unavoidable Masonic commitments, the first of which was at the Holborn Restaurant on the 26th October 1889, with the Earl of Latham in the Chair. Also present, seated alongside fellow Grand Lodge Representative Bro. Michael Maybrick, was City of London Police Doctor, Bro. Gordon Brown, attendant at the murder of Mary Ann Kelly in Mitre Square, and assistant at the autopsy of Alice Mackenzie. Michael Maybrick, quietly revelling in the irony of the doctor's company, was called upon to sing the solo verses of the National Anthem that evening, in the course of which casual conversation would have included word of the resolute police officer in charge of the Whitechapel investigations, Inspector Frederick George Abberline, having recently been proposed as a candidate for initiation into the mysteries and privileges of Ancient Freemasonry, scheduled for early December. The jolly baritone Michael Maybrick would have had much on his mind during the journey home.

On the 4th December 1889, Frederick Abberline was duly initiated into Zetland Lodge No.511, at Anderson's Hotel, Fleet Street, London, during which ceremony Abberline would have been 'divested of all metals' including rings, and would have been warned, in no uncertain manner, of the dire ritual consequences of betraying the brotherhood, chillingly similar to the treatment meted out to the victims of the Whitechapel Murderer. By the end of the evening, Bro. Abberline's mind had entered a new dimension.

Michael Maybrick's next Masonic commitment was the traditional Festival of St. John the Divine, held annually on the 27th December at United Grand Lodge, Great Queen Street, London, on which occasion Bro. Maybrick would have received an overtly fraternal welcome, bolstering his confidence, and reinforcing the belief that all was not lost. Less than ten days later, he made his first public appearance at the annual London Ballad Concert at St. James's Hall, Piccadilly, organised by the wine loving impresario John Boosey, an event high on the social listings, with an invited audience guaranteed to impart a favourable reception.

Mr. Michael Maybrick, the well-known vocalist, and, under the nom-de-plume of Stephen Adams, an equally known composer, made his re-appearance at a ballad concert in London on Saturday, for the first time since the Maybrick Trial, in which he was a principal witness. The sympathy of his admirers was expressed by a most cordial reception accorded to him in his appearance on the platform at the St. James's Hall, to sing his own song, 'A Little Hero', and the

applause was repeated with even greater warmth at the conclusion of the song for the encore, to which Mr. Maybrick substituted his own ballad, 'They All Love Jack'
Aberdeen Evening Express. 7 January 1890.

The parting jibe was irresistible, flaunting his secret infamy, mocking the world, 'I am Jack!' The deluded fools didn't have a clue. One week later, with triumphal self-belief fully restored, a public relations exercise was contrived in the form of a interview with a sycophantic reporter from 'The World' magazine.

There are few houses between Portland Place and Hampstead Heath which command a finer view from the upper windows than the provokingly angular brick buildings at the north-west corner of Regent's Park, dignified by the name of Wellington Mansions. Dwellers in Wellington Mansions are accustomed to regulate their clocks by Big Ben, and a tradition exists among them that on exceptionally clear days they can catch a sight of Windsor Castle. 'Pleasant melodies must have pleasant surroundings' was a favourite axiom of Stephen Adams, long before he set all England singing with such familiar airs as 'Nancy Lee', 'The Midshipmite', and 'They All Love Jack'. The chimes of a clock have scarcely died away before you turn into a sunny room, where the stalwart lieutenant of the 'Artists' is at work before a table littered with quill pens, and almost as many boxes of cigars and cigarettes. As he talks to you of the last Easter Artists manoeuvres, or of the next meeting of the Grand Lodge, for Stephen Adams has risen to the Masonic Rank of Grand Organist, he runs his hands involuntarily over the keys, but the stirring chorus you listen to is not that of the 'Entered Apprentice', but the potential lineal successor of

'They All Love Jack'. He possesses the muscle and brawn of an ideal Life Guardsman, and his passion for every form of outdoor pursuit has enabled him to retain the full figure of youth much longer than his contemporaries. When Stephen Adams is not working, he is either drilling at Somerset House, imbibing ozone at his Isle of Wight cottage, rowing on the Thames, riding on Highgate Hill, or engaging the conviviality of the Arts Club. Michael Maybrick puts his whole strength into everything he does. He regards his exercise out of doors and the social evenings he spends at one or other of his clubs as the most welcome preparation for his labours at home.

The World. 15 January 1890.

Two days later, on the 17th January, Michael Maybrick performed on stage in Hull, followed by attendance at occasional Masonic functions, but his popularity had waned, and it soon became evident that the glory days were over. Fortuitously, over the previous few months, interest in events surrounding the Maybrick Trial had been superseded by the public's insatiable appetite for fresh gossip, with none more savoury than that involving Royalty.

CLEVELAND STREET

In late 1889, a scandal erupted within London society, centred around a police raid, led by Inspector Frederick Abberline, on a homosexual paedophile brothel in Cleveland Street, Westminster, frequented by clients ranging from the military to aristocracy. Deliberately orchestrated delays by the Establishment resulted in the more influential suspects escaping arrest, leaving the lower strata of clientele to face charges. The public was not only shocked at the existence of such premises, but incensed at the inequality of treatment meted out to the participants.

Lord Arthur Somerset, Equerry to HRH the Prince of Wales, fled to Europe, the Earl of Euston left the country amidst rumours of his departure to Peru, and the main witness for the prosecution, brothel keeper Charles Hammond, was spirited away to France. Prince Albert Victor, 'Prince Eddy', was not on the premises at the time of the raid, but reliable sources soon confirmed that the Prince had been an attendee on a number of occasions. Unsurprisingly, the British newspapers displayed a marked reluctance to comment on the matter in any depth, but the American press displayed no such hesitancy.

The number involved is variously stated as from sixteen to forty, and the names that are mentioned embrace even royalty, but tremendous efforts are being made to shield the titled culprits from exposure. Only one name of that class, that of Lord Somerset, is given with certainty, and he was allowed to get away. Current rumour says that Prince Albert

will not return from India until the matter is completely over and forgotten.
New York Times. 10 March 1889.

It is obvious to everybody that there has come to be, within the last few days, a general conviction that this long-necked, narrow-minded young dullard was mixed up in the scandal, and out of this had sprung a half whimsical notion, which one hears propounded now about clubland, that matters will be so arranged that he will never return from India. What this really mirrors is a public awakening to the fact that this stupid perverse boy has become a man, and has only two precious lives between him and the English throne
New York Times. 17 November 1889.

The Maybrick Trial faded into relative insignificance alongside events ensuing from the Cleveland Street scandal, but a warning bell had been sounded. Social unease heightened as reputable gentlemen of long-standing bachelor status were regarded in a different light, with no-one more suspect in the public eye than Prince Eddy, whose future conduct from this point onwards would be guided, in no uncertain manner, by unseen elements within the hierarchy. The bachelor prince was destined to marry, although the bride had yet to be determined.

The Prince's first potential match was selected within weeks, in the form of Princess Alex of Hesse, whose outright refusal of Eddy's proposal of engagement demonstrated not only the Princess's laudable independence of spirit, but the artificiality of such arranged marriages. Princess Alex went on to marry Tsar Nicholas Romanoff, Emperor of Russia, subsequently meeting a grisly end when the whole family was executed by the Bolsheviks in the Russian Revolution.

The second potential love match followed two months later, hastily convened with Princess Helene of Orleans, but this arrangement floundered on political differences and religious incompatibility, following which, over the next few months, the Prince dallied with a chorus girl from the Gaiety Theatre, serving to some extent to counter-balance rumours still in circulation around his involvement in the Cleveland Street scandal.

Romance finally blossomed in 1891, with Princess May of Teck, to whom the Prince became engaged, with the wedding set for 1892. At the same time as Eddy was being married off to accord with convention, Eddy's tutor, J.K. Stephen, also decided to seek a wife, conveniently selected, with little consultation, in the form of his cousin, Stella Duckworth, but unsurprisingly the match was not to be, resulting in a serious bout of mental depression. In searching for a wife, Stephen was evidently doing what was expected, but his true sentiments are reflected in poems penned shortly after the romance that never was.

I do not want to see that girl again,
I did not like her, and I shall not mind,
If she were done away with, killed or ploughed,
She did not serve a useful end,
And certainly she was not beautiful.

J.K. Stephen. The Backs.

Stella Duckworth was a fortunate lady. In December 1891, James Kenneth Stephen was admitted to a private mental asylum, where, on hearing that Prince Eddy had been taken ill, his health began to deteriorate. When the news was announced, on the 14th January 1892, that Prince Albert Edward Victor had died unexpectedly, Stephen refused to eat, dying twenty days later, aged 32. Prince Eddy's betrothed, Princess Mary of Teck, promptly courted and became engaged to his younger brother George, now next in line to the throne after the Prince of Wales, eventually becoming King George V and Queen Mary, grandparents to Queen Elizabeth II.

In Victorian England, the average age for marriage was 26 for men, and 24 for women, statistics which mattered little to the disinterested bachelor of the time, but public perception would change after Cleveland Street. Michael and Edwin were 49 and 39 respectively in 1890, and the decision was taken, reluctantly, to conform to traditional values, and minimise further scrutiny by public and press. In early 1891 Edwin returned to Merseyside, taking up lodgings in Wallasey, a burgeoning seaside town opposite Liverpool on the River Mersey, linked by a regular ferry service to the city. In the National Census of 1891, Edwin is listed as a boarder at Eaton Villas, Rowson Street, where also resided Miss Amy Tyrer, Lodging House Keeper, aged 31. In the same census, brother William is listed in Wellington Road, Wallasey, only 250 yards away. This fortuitous and carefully manoeuvred arrangement has all the hallmarks of Michael's guiding hand, freeing himself from Edwin by returning him to work at the Cotton Exchange, leaving him secure in the proximity of brother William, and even closer proximity of his unattached landlady.

THE HOLY CITY

In 1892, having weathered the swell of unpopularity following those adverse press reports, Michael Maybrick, in a moment of divine inspiration, experienced a spiritual visitation, an ethereal vision, which he felt compelled to transcribe into musical form .... *'last night as I lay sleeping, there came a dream so fair ... methought the voice of angels from heaven in answer rang.'* His old musical partner Fred Weatherly immediately agreed to collaborate in the composition, and the pair set about transforming the divine message into one of the most iconic anthems the world has known, 'The Holy City', selling over a million copies of sheet music, and revered to the present day.

Michael Maybrick had experienced salvation, and life would change thereafter. Bolstered by new wealth from the endless flow of royalties, the now feted celebrity moved from the Regent's Park apartment to an impressive detached residence in Wellington Road, St. John's Wood, opting against a return to the stage, in favour of a more leisurely lifestyle.

The next phase of this Damascene conversion would be the reluctant transition from bachelor status to the bliss of married life, following in the footsteps of his younger brother. The first person to whom he looked was housekeeper Laura Withers, a butcher's daughter with no pretences, ten years his junior, an ideal arrangement, without the involvement of gratuitous romance.

Meanwhile, Bro. Frederick Abberline, on the first spoke of the Masonic ladder, had been spending many an hour contemplating, correlating, and re-assessing the Whitechapel Murders in a different light. Missing pieces of the jig-saw were falling into place, with all the evidence indicating that the murderer was a Freemason, although there was little he could do about it. Back in December 1890, one year after his initiation into Freemasonry, Abberline had been promoted to the rank of Chief Inspector, yet in February 1892, less than eighteen months later, he resigned from the Metropolitan Police, 'for undisclosed reasons.' What could have prompted this resolute detective to quit the force, well before retirement age? Was he issued with a directive which conflicted with his personal convictions, to cast aside the more obvious leads to a satisfactory conclusion? The exposure of Jack the Ripper as a Freemason would have resulted in disastrous repercussions within the Establishment, representing a very real threat to national stability. Were vested interests afoot to keep the truth under wraps?

Abberline's handwritten notes on the murder of Mary Jane Kelly finish with the line, 'I was advised not to pursue any more into this investigation.' Almost fifty years after his death, an intriguing interview during Abberline's retirement years was recollected in the following newspaper report, with a clear reference to his Masonic vow of silence.

'I have given my word to keep my mouth permanently closed about it. I know, my superiors know, certain facts ....you'd have to look for him, not at the bottom of London society, but a long way up.'

Evening News. 26 June 1976.

One superior of note was Chief Inspector Bro. John Littlechild, a member of Bro. Abberline's own Zetland Lodge No.511, Head of the Irish Division of Special Branch, charged with the suppression of insurrection, with a direct remit to the Lord Chamberlain, Bro. The Earl of Lathom, personal adviser to HM Queen Victoria.

Bro. Abberline had evidently arrived at the conclusion that an arrest would never take place, signalling his muted objection by taking early retirement, followed by employment with the European branch of the Pinkerton Detective Agency.

Whilst the Government was doing all in its power to silence Florence Maybrick, barrister Alexander MacDougall was doing his best to secure her release, championing the cause with the publication, in the summer of 1892, of a magnificent 600 page treatise, 'The Maybrick Case. A Treatise on the Facts of the Case, and of the Proceedings in Connection with the Charge, Trial, Conviction and Present Imprisonment of

Florence Maybrick.' The book includes transcripts of court proceedings, deeply opinionated commentary upon police and judicial irregularities, and unrelenting emphasis on the suspicious behaviour of Michael Maybrick.

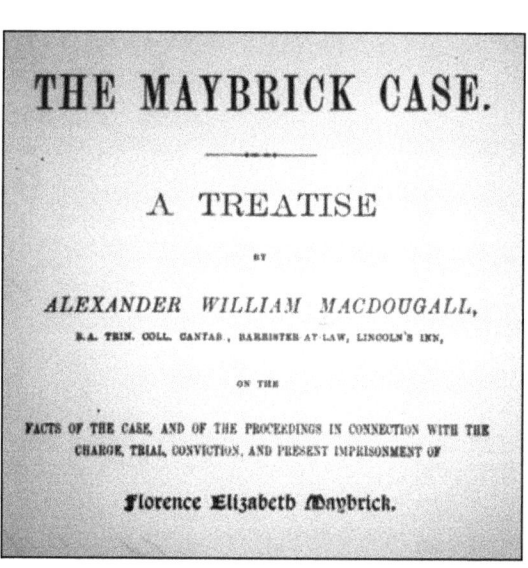

In this Maybrick case, from first to last, the question has been of suspicious circumstances we have had to deal with. Now, suspicion itself is a nasty idea. There is, in the very word, a sibilation which reminds one of the hissing of a snake in the grass, and it is the first instinct of a healthy mind, when the word suspicion is heard, to look for the snake in the grass. It is a sort of instruction, which warns us, when we hear of persons being suspected, to enquire who suspects. And those who suspect others must expect to be suspected themselves. My readers will entertain no doubt that there is something behind all this, that there was some puller behind the scenes, some 'snake in the grass' who can answer the question which is the real mystery of the Maybrick case, How, why, and by

whom was the charge of murdering put upon Mrs. Maybrick? I venture to think that my readers will agree with me that there are 'suspicious circumstances' which point away from a murderer, and point towards some unfriendly person, who was seeking to put a charge on Mrs. Maybrick.

Alexander MacDougall.

This was no 'Mr. R.F. Muckley,' readily intimidated by the threat of libel action, but an extremely competent and assertive barrister on a mission, throwing down the gauntlet, and inviting a response. Inspired by MacDougall's crusade, on the other side of the Atlantic, Helen Densmore was also hot on the trail of the Maybrick brothers, jousting in correspondence with the editor of 'The Hawk' magazine.

The Messrs. Maybrick have, after many weeks delay, deigned to give the information that all and every statement which refers to themselves, and which appear in print, is without foundation. The Editor of The Hawk accepts unreservedly these statements, oblivious to the fact that the Messrs. Maybrick are not disinterested parties, they are of the 'five unfriendly persons' whom Mr. MacDougall says were permitted by the police to roam over the house, and assist them in search of material for putting on Mrs. Maybrick a charge of murdering her husband. Indeed, the editor ignores the fact that, before the public, the Maybrick brothers are quite as much on trial as Mrs. Maybrick. There is seen, in all this, the trail of the same serpent that has followed this case from the first. The conspiracy commenced before Mr. Maybrick was dead. It followed Mrs. Maybrick to prison, where she was remanded before there was even any well-grounded suspicion of her guilt. The police were called in, and shown by the inmates the arsenic scattered throughout the house. These inmates knew all the places where it was to be found, and there exists not a particle of evidence to show that it was in the house before Mr. Maybrick died. The

suspects trail followed her into the dock, and it has continued to wind its slimy folds along the path during the past three years of her fateful life, wherever and whenever an effort is made for her release.
Helen Densmore. The Maybrick Case 1892.

Michael Maybrick appeared superficially undeterred by these continuous onslaughts, but, in late 1892, with housekeeper Laura Withers in tow, moved lock, stock and barrel from their new abode in St. John's Wood to the Isle of Wight, effectively breaking all ties with London society. No explanation was ever proffered for this seemingly odd course of action.

In December, 1892, doubtless spurred on by brother Michael, Edwin married his landlady, Amy Tyrer, at the Islington Registry Office, and moved from Wallasey back across the River Mersey to Waterloo, on the outskirts of Liverpool, where he resumed work at the Liverpool Exchange.

Arrangements were set in place for Michael's own wedding early the following year but, there was one matter, concerning snippets of small talk picked up by Edwin at the Liverpool Exchange, which would prove disastrous should a particular individual decide to make contact with that relentlessly persistent barrister, Alexander MacDougall.

In early February, 1893, Michael Maybrick travelled over 200 miles to the North of England, where, on the 9th, he appeared at the Assembly Rooms, Hull, as one of a number of artists in supporting roles to the principal attraction, Mr. Edward Lloyd. A strange course of action for a man resolved to avoid further public appearances. The concert was not particularly well received.

CONCERT IN HULL

Contrary to expectation, the audience in the Assembly Rooms last night was not so large as expected. Mr. Edward Lloyd was the principal attraction. The principal tenor was a little hoarse, but, nonetheless, the success of his singing of 'The Holy City' was very marked. The favourable impression created by Mr. Maybrick when last in Hull was evidently well remembered by the audience. It is a question, however, whether he is appreciated more as 'Stephen Adams' the composer, or as Mr. Maybrick, the baritone.

Hull Daily Mail. 10 February 1893.

In other words, you are not as popular as you were, Mr. Maybrick, best concentrate on composing. Just the reaction anticipated by friends and colleagues three years earlier, on his tentative return to public life, after the self-imposed exile on the Isle of Wight. Why then travel such a great distance, at the risk of such a response? Had Michael combined the trip to Hull with a prior visit to brother Edwin, now living in Waterloo, only five miles from Liverpool? Had George Davidson been talking too much at the Liverpool Exchange, where Edwin also worked? Had a decision been made, following which Michael boarded the train from Liverpool to Hull, firmly establishing his whereabouts, 130 miles away.

Confirmation of his presence in Hull that night would certainly provide an alibi for the night in question. London of course, would have been preferable, but circumstances had dictated a face-to-face meeting with Edwin.

That same night George Davidson, James Maybrick's lifelong friend, and joint signatory to James's controversial will, disappeared in mysterious circumstances. His body had evidently been carried by tidal currents from the Mersey

Estuary into the Irish Sea, to be discovered four weeks later, washed up on a wind-swept beach in Cumberland, eighty miles away. Davidson's close friend, James Stewart, issued the following statement at the inquest.

'I was an old friend of the deceased, and had known him for twenty three years. The deceased had been missing since about February 10th, and a reward of £10 was being offered for information about him. I last saw the deceased alive about four o'clock on the afternoon of February 9th, in the Liverpool Exchange. He dined at 6.30 on the evening February 9th, and afterwards went to bed, but his landlady thought she heard the front door close about 12.30 on the morning of the 10th. About 10.00 a.m. he was found to be missing, and has not since been heard of. It was a wild stormy night, and it is supposed this is the reason why he put on old clothes. The deceased was a strong minded man, and not one at all likely to commit suicide, and, as far as I know, there was nothing in his state of his affairs which would lead him to do so. The deceased lived about one and a quarter miles from the docks. We cannot account in any way for his getting in the water.'

Millom News. 11 March 1893.

THE DISAPPEARANCE OF A COTTON BROKER.

BODY FOUND.

Private information to hand enables us to say that the body of Mr. Davidson, who has been missing just four weeks to-day, was found yesterday at Millom, where the body had been cast on the shore. A very great friend of the deceased recognised the body, and at the inquest held to-day a verdict of "Found drowned" was returned. The interment takes place in Cumberland to-morrow (Friday).

THE DECEASED GENTLEMAN
AND THE MAYBRICK CASE

With reference to the fate of the late Mr. Davidson, a correspondent writes ...... 'One of the remarkable stories connected with another Liverpool mystery is the absence from the witness box at Mrs. Maybrick's trial of this same George R. Davidson. He was Mr. James Maybrick's most intimate friend; a bed was always ready at his house, and constantly occupied by this same Mr. George R. Davidson, and during Mr. James Maybrick's illness, he was constantly at his bedside, and the dying man expired in his arms .... Mr. George R. Davidson was absent from the witness box, a fact that may have meant nothing, but which has been much commented on by Mr. Alexander MacDougall, and those who have laboured to secure a re-opening of the case.'

South Wales Echo. 11 March 1893.

TILL DEATH US DO PART

Michael Maybrick, Mayor of Ryde, Isle of Wight.

On the 7th March 1893, two days prior to the opening of the inquest in Cumberland on George Davidson, three hundred miles away in a Registry Office in Marylebone, London, Michael Maybrick took Laura Withers to be his lawful wedded wife, 'till death us do part', a time constraint regarded by the groom as a variable factor, should the need arise. This had been not so much a marriage of souls as a marriage of convenience, without the inconvenience of romantic involvement, yet whilst Laura may well have harboured misgivings over her master's orientation and strange behaviour, there had never been any doubting her total loyalty. The principal witness to this loveless match was none other than Dr. Charles Fuller, appointed by Michael Maybrick as guardian of Florence's children, Bobo and Gladys, now in London, close to Michael, ensuring their mother's continued silence.

So what had induced Michael Maybrick's unaccountable departure from the newly acquired residence in St. John's Wood? Bro. The Earl of Lathom had been closely following the critical press reports on Bro. Maybrick's conduct in events surrounding the death of his brother James, and had studied in depth Alexander MacDougall's recently published and much acclaimed treatise on the Trial of Florence Maybrick. Such conduct was unbecoming of a high ranking Freemason, and the matter would have to be rectified. Furthermore, following the murder of Alice Mackenzie, it was quite evident that Jack the Ripper was alive and well, completely negating Bro. Maybrick's confidentially disclosed suspicions that his now deceased brother James could well have been involved in the Whitechapel murders. All very strange, as were the circumstances concerning the unjustified imprisonment of Florence Maybrick, in which Bro. Michael Maybrick had played such a prominent role. Pieces of this very odd jigsaw puzzle were beginning to fall into place.

It is a sort of intuition which warns us, when we hear of persons being suspected, to enquire 'who suspects', and

those who suspect others must expect to be suspected themselves.
Alexander MacDougall.

At the same time, Bros. Abberline and Littlechild had been mulling over the circumstantial evidence surrounding the mysterious tall man prone to disguise, with the finger of suspicion moving in the direction of one particular member of a Whitechapel Vigilance Association, able to blend into the community unnoticed. Various options were available to Bro. Littlechild, as Head of the Irish Division of Special Branch, and well versed in subterfuge, but the suspect was a fellow Freemason in high office and very well connected. There were certainly strong grounds for suspicion, but proof was totally lacking. Whatever exchanges took place behind closed doors will never be known, but in late 1892 Michael Maybrick, faced with an offer he could not refuse, the prospect of exclusion or honourable retirement, reluctantly tendered his resignation from St. George's Chapter 42 of the Ancient and Accepted Rite, and left London for a new life on the Isle of Wight, maintaining his allegiance to Freemasonry, but ending his mainland involvement with the Order, and seething with an incandescent but futile craving for revenge.

'I believe if chance prevails I will burn St James's to the ground'
The Diary of Jack the Ripper, Shirley Harrison.

This complete change of direction may well have alleviated the psychiatric problems which had surfaced in Whitechapel. The crucial trigger situations simply did not exist in this new environment, and the successful completion of the Funny Little Games had exorcised the traumatic adolescent experience. The problem had ceased to exist. The

Whitechapel Murders were a secret suspected but unproven by a small number of influential Freemasons. No-one would ever decipher his clever little clues. The matter was now closed. Still feted for his masterpiece, 'The Holy City', the newlywed was now in his element, firmly ensconced in the family residence, Lynthorpe, from whence he would routinely emerge in a pristine black coach and pair, the doors of which were inscribed with the Maybrick crest and motto, 'Tempus Revelat Omnia', ...'Time Reveals All'.

Lynthorpe, Isle of Wight.

Whilst Michael Maybrick was intent on promoting a popular image of geniality and bonhomie, Edwin's daughter Amy, recalling time spent visiting Lynthorpe as a child, provides a more revealing insight into the man behind the image.

Michael wasn't fond of children, and didn't want anything to do with them. All the Maybricks were very cold, very formal.

The house itself was cold, heated in winter by an oil-stove of some kind in the dining room. She remembers her uncle as vain, arrogant, dictatorial, and bereft of friends.

They All Love Jack. Bruce Robinson.

From the moment of his establishing residency, the populace of Ryde had embraced the flamboyant celebrity, paving the way for the next phase in the life of this extraordinary man, now wholeheartedly determined to further his social standing within the community, which comprised many distinguished individuals. For the previous fifty years, Osborne House in East Cowes had been the rural summer retreat of HM Queen Victoria, as a consequence of which the island had attracted some very influential residents, an irresistible challenge for the new arrival, well versed in the art of social advancement. Michael Maybrick soon became deeply embroiled in local politics, and within seven years was elected Mayor and Chief Magistrate of Ryde, a position to which he would be re-elected on a further five occasions.

In February 1897, Michael Maybrick joined Ryde Lodge No. 698, which would henceforth be his sole involvement with Freemasonry.

In 1904, on expiry of the fifteen year sentence arbitrarily imposed by Home Secretary Henry Matthews, Florence Maybrick was released from prison. In anticipation of this event, five years earlier, in 1899, guardianship of the children had been transferred from Dr. Fuller, whose surname they had legally adopted, into the custody of their uncle Michael in the Isle of Wight, 'in furtherance of their wellbeing'. Florence's continued silence and tacit co-operation was assured. One year later, just after his eighteenth birthday, James left for a new life in America, whilst Gladys remained at Lynthorpe, eventually marrying a naval officer.

Immediately following release from confinement, Florence sailed to America, to be greeted by a loyal band of supporters, who arranged a series of lecture tours, ensuring financial stability for a while. Hard times followed, however, and Florence spent the remainder of her life as a recluse, in the company of her precious cats. Florence had last embraced her precious children, Bobo and Gladys, in May 1888, the week Michael Maybrick had arrived in Battlecrease House. Florence never saw them again, dying alone and penniless in Connecticut, buried along with her secrets, under a small stone marker, in a pauper's grave.

In July, 1913, Michael Maybrick's health deteriorated, and, after a period of recuperation at a health spa in Buxton, Derbyshire, he died suddenly on the 26th August. His body was conveyed without delay back to the Isle of Wight, where, on 30th August, 1913, a resplendent funeral ceremony was organised, attended by Alfred Lord Tennyson, representing HRH Princess Beatrice, Governor of the Isle of Wight.

Funeral procession of Michael Maybrick.

The funeral of the late Michael Maybrick, J.P. took place at Ryde on Saturday, amidst universal tokens of sorrow. There was hardly a business establishment in the town which did not display some signs of mourning, while the flags on the public buildings were lowered to half-mast. A correspondent with a very long experience of public obsequences on the island writes that he has never seen so large an attendance, manifesting such evident signs of grief for a personal loss.

Isle of Wight County Press. 6 September 1913.

Significantly, despite Michael Maybrick's distinguished Masonic career, and the scale of his funeral arrangements, the attendance list reveals the only Freemasons present were members of the local Ryde Lodge.

Two days after Michael Maybrick's death, the following article appeared in the Manchester Courier, announcing the death of Bernard Quaritch, the day immediately after Michael Maybrick.

The death occurred yesterday, at Brighton, of Mr. Bernard Quaritch, head of the famous London firm of booksellers. Mr. Quaritch, who was in his forty third year, had been ailing for a long time, and had never recovered from an illness which overtook him on a visit to America in 1911.

Manchester Courier. 28th August 1913.

Yet another 'coincidence' in the ongoing saga of Michael Maybrick, with more to follow. One week later, the Isle of Wight County Press published a lengthy article on proceedings at the funeral, detailing all dignitaries, individuals and organisations present. An addenda to the article reads as follows,

A correspondent of the Daily Telegraph writes, It is a curious fact the late Mr. Quaritch, the prince of booksellers, and the late Mr. Maybrick were both members of 'B' Company of the Artists Corps of Volunteers together, and left the Corps about the same time, some 20 years ago. They were both buried at the same time on Saturday.

Isle of Wight County Press. 6 September 1913.

The substance of this article would seem to have emanated from a conversation between the local reporter and Lieutenant Colonel H. May, on the attendance list as representing the regiment at the funeral. Evidently Michael Maybrick and Bernard Quaritch not only joined the Artists Rifles at the same time, but resigned together, at a time coinciding with Maybrick's move from London to the Isle of Wight. Quaritch, a life-long bachelor, died mysteriously on the 27th August, the day after Maybrick, with the funeral organised to coincide on the same day, the 30th August. Arrangements must have been in place for his immediate notification in the event of Maybrick's death, as on the following day news had not yet been released to the press.

Theirs was evidently a very close relationship, extending through the Whitechapel Murders and the period of exile in the Isle of Wight, the likely time of origin for the Maybrick diary. To what extent had this young man been involved in Maybrick's secret world?

Twenty seventh August 1913 Lynton Lodge New Church Road Alvington	Bernard Alfred Quaritch	Male	42 years	Antiquarian Bookseller	(1) Chronic Interstitial nephritis (2) Uraemic poisoning Cardiac synopsis Certified by J.J. Eccles

Bernard Quaritch's Death Certificate relates the cause of death as 'Chronic Interstitial Nephritis. Uraemic poisoning. Cardiac synopsis.' A carefully worded diagnosis by the lifelong family doctor, from which may be deduced 'death from overdose of prescriptive medicine,' avoiding any embarrassing reference to suicide. Suicide within twenty four hours of the death of Michael Maybrick. who was laid to rest in a vaulted marble grave, on the side of which was engraved 'There Shall Be No More Death'. On the day of the internment, a poignant finale to that eventful week was published in The Globe.

Mr. F.E. Weatherly, the famous songwriter, who wrote the words for many of the famous ballads composed by Stephen Adams, (Mr. Michael Maybrick), who died at the beginning of the week, sends the following. 'The last song of a large number written for my dear friend Stephen Adams. We little thought the end was so near.'

FRIEND OF MINE
When you are happy, friend of mine,
And all your skies are blue,

Tell me your luck, your fortune fine,
And let me laugh with you.
Tell me the hopes that spur you on,
The deeds you mean to do.
The gold you've struck, the fame you've won,
And let me joy, - with you.
When you are sad, and heart acold,
And all your skies are dark,
Tell me the dreams that mocked your hold,
The shafts that missed the mark,
Am I not yours for real or woe?
How else can friends prove true!
Tell me what breaks and brings you low,
And let me stand with you.
So when the night falls tremulous,
When the last lamp burns low,
And one of us, or both of us,
The long lone road must go.
Look with your dear old eyes in mine,
Give me a handshake true,
Whatever fate, our souls await,
Let me be there – with you.

EPILOGUE

In 1992, Michael Maybrick's contrived diary was discovered in Liverpool, and it was widely accepted, as intended, that the contents implicated James Maybrick as Jack the Ripper. Whilst investigations for the main part were based around the alleged association with Battlecrease House, or the veracity of the various parties involved in the discovery, researchers Paul Feldman and Keith Skinner decided to direct their enquiries around the recollections of the father of one of those parties. Billy Graham, 80 years old, was interviewed at length in 1993 in a series of recorded conversations, included in which was the revelation that his grandmother Elizabeth had accompanied Alice Yapp to the Maybrick Trial.

'Well, they talked about it for years, they all talked about it, when she came to Liverpool, and my grandmother went with the skivvy. She was the one that opened the letter and she went to the Assizes – everyone talked about it – big licks it was – everyone was dashing up to buy a newspaper, and half of them couldn't read or write.

Jack the Ripper. The Final Chapter. Paul Feldman.

Billy was seemingly oblivious to the import of this revelation, a clear reference to Alice Yapp, 'the skivvy that opened the letter', imparted in such a credible and matter of fact way. Believers in the authenticity of the Diary assumed James Maybrick to be the Whitechapel Murderer, but in the light of Alice Yapp's deep involvement with Michael Maybrick, the final pieces of the jigsaw begin to fall into place, especially when Billy's next disclosure was the long standing family rumour that Florence Maybrick had conceived a child in her teenage years, whilst in Hartlepool, on the east coast of England. This child, named William, was purportedly Billy's father, born in 1878. At the time of the interview, Billy was in poor health, and died the following year, in 1994.

So how long had Alice Yapp, no friend of Florence Maybrick, been a friend of the family of Florence's illegitimate offspring? At the time of the Maybrick Trial, in 1889, Alice was 26 years old and grandmother Elizabeth 39, and according to Billy Graham's recollection of the story, the pair had attended the trial together. Had Florence been illicitly supporting the child, and had Elizabeth, following Florence's arrest, made contact, in good faith, with James's brother Michael, the only person who may possibly have assisted in the upkeep of the child ? Walk this way, said the spider to the fly.

Nothing could have pleased Michael Maybrick more than the perverse satisfaction of this deeply shocking revelation in puritanical Victorian times, knowledge of which would henceforth ensure Florence's total compliance, just as the Trial was about to commence. Did Florence, gazing round the faces in St. George's Hall, stare incomprehensively at Elizabeth and Alice Yapp, seated together. Impossible. This must be Michael Maybrick's doing. Could this account for Florence's demeanour when Michael Maybrick took the stand, and for Lord Russell's inexplicably lenient treatment of Michael and Edwin during the Trial, if such were his client's instructions?

Alice Yapp, for her part, had proved totally loyal to Michael Maybrick, resolute in her adherence to their fabricated story, and had been the ideal person to befriend Billy Graham's grandmother Elizabeth. Alice Yapp would be the custodian of

Michael Maybrick's Diary, with instructions to 'discover' it in the unlikely event of Michael's arrest as Jack the Ripper. Diligent planning and contingency arrangements had always been intrinsic to Michael's duplicitous mindset, and what better final retribution than to arrange for Alice Yapp, following Michael's death, to pass on the shameful Diary to the family of Florence's illegitimate offspring, revealing Florence, the wife of Jack the Ripper, to be their matriarch.

Ironically, the recipient, Elizabeth, was illiterate, and the diary remained unread, placed in a cupboard with other household items, and left there for many years. According to Billy,

'I used to draw her pension for her, she couldn't read or write, so she used to put a cross on her pension book.'
Jack the Ripper. The Final Chapter. Paul Feldman.

Fifteen years prior to the discovery of the Diary in 1991, totally unaware of the link with the Graham family, author Neil Morland related Florence Maybrick's move from Aylesbury Prison on expiry of her sentence.

.....in January of that year was moved from Aylesbury Prison to the House of Epiphany on the banks of the Fal in Cornwall, where, as Mrs. Graham, she was to try and regain some of her former health and strength.
Neil Morland. The Friendless Lady.

No-one could understand why, on her release from prison, Florence had adopted the name Graham, but Billy Graham's family secret now provides the answer. At the time of the interview, Keith Skinner made the following observation,

'I recalled Florence Aunspaugh's description of Florence Maybrick's eyes. Mrs. Maybrick's eyes were the most beautiful blue I have ever seen. They were large round eyes

and such a very deep blue that at times they were violet. Just like Billy Graham's'.

Jack the Ripper. The Final Chapter. Paul Feldman.

In 1927, Florence made an unannounced visit back to England, as reported in the Liverpool Post and Mercury.

Mrs. Florence Elizabeth Maybrick, who in 1889 was sentenced to death for poisoning her husband, a wealthy stockbroker, has been re-visiting Liverpool, where the scenes of the notorious drama were set. The sentence was commuted to penal servitude for life, and Mrs. Maybrick was released some years ago, when she went to live with her mother in America. Unknown to anyone save the solicitor and a few personal friends, Mrs. Maybrick, the central figure in one of the most sensational poison dramas of our time, had just concluded a brief visit to England, and the only interview she gave during her stay is published exclusively below.

MAYBRICK DRAMA
SECRET VISIT TO LIVERPOOL
MRS. MAYBRICK AT OLD SCENES
HOPES OF REUNION WITH FAMILY

Sad faced, gentle voiced, with hair turned to silver, the Mrs. Maybrick of today is but a shadow of the striking looking woman who made a lasting impression on those who saw her in the dock in Liverpool 37 years ago. 'I feel death's shadow over me, and I have come back with one object only, to effect a reconciliation with members of my family, if that be possible..... All the years that have passed since the terrible day when I heard the verdict of guilt, I have longed for my children, who were but babes at the time, and the mother hunger in my heart was so strong that I feel I must make this journey now, in the hope of seeing them.'

Though disappointed in the main object of her visit to the scenes of early life in England, Mrs. Maybrick was not disposed to give up readily. She is turning her attention to following up new points bearing on her innocence, and has managed with a private enquiry agent to go over the ground in the hope of securing corroboration of several points, which, it is contended, strongly suggest her innocence. 'If the new enquiries bear fruit and produce the evidence necessary to establish my innocence, I shall return to England to make one last attempt at reconciliation, for death without the forgiveness of my children for all the unhappiness I have brought them through my folly would be terrible.'

Pressed as to what she meant by her folly, Mrs. Maybrick said, 'I mean the love affair that played such a big part in the case against me. There were circumstances at home that drove me into the arms of another man, and I was foolish enough to think that I could find happiness with the man who offered the love my husband denied me. Bitterly, I have repented ever since.'

Liverpool Post & Mercury. 2 May 1927.

Florence must have been aware that her son James had died in a tragic accident sixteen years earlier, leaving Gladys the only surviving child, yet Florence unequivocally refers in the article to the hope of seeing her 'children', which, in the light of Billy Graham's statement, is now open to conjecture.

One major barrier to authenticity of the newly discovered diary had been reference to the Poste House, an alehouse which, according to critics, did not exist in Liverpool at the time of the Whitechapel Murders. This anomaly has now been resolved in the opening chapter of this book, considerably enhancing the credibility of the Diary.

The handwriting, however, bears no resemblance to that of either James or Michael, taught in the same school by the same English master, and distinctly similar in style. It has been convincingly argued that a schizophrenic undergoing a personality change can write in totally alien style, but the consistency in script could not have been maintained on a daily basis throughout duration of the diary, and a more credible assumption is that the script is a later copy of the original, written in the handwriting of the perpetrator, in the fair assumption at the time that no evidence existed of James Maybrick's handwriting.

The content is a combination of both Maybrick brothers, murderously vengeful and uncontrollably psychotic, yet sharp, witty and mischievous in the manner of the alter-ego balladeer, whilst frustrated and ultimately remorseful in a manner more suited to a genuinely ailing conscience-stricken philanderer. A skilfully integrated blend of diligently doctored entries from James's diary, interwoven into the carefully contrived journal of a crazed contemptuous killer. Two diaries in one, a manipulation of fact, fantasy and deception, in which Michael Maybrick assumes the mantle of 'Sir Jim', in substitute for 'Sir Michael', subliminally craving a knighthood, an ambition which would never have entered the mind of cotton broker James Maybrick.

Interspersed within the rambling dialogue are occasional Maybrick red herrings, mischievous clues leading anywhere but the right direction, randomly out of context, and a source of merriment to the perpetrator, so superior, so infinitely more intelligent than the reader struggling in vain to interpret the input of these incongruous asides.

'I have taken up lodgings in Middlesex Street, that in itself is a joke', as bold a reference to the 20th Middlesex(Artists Rifles) as *'Maybee'* was to Maybrick and Toynbee Hall.

'Mrs Hammersmith is a whore.' Despite intensive research, the identity of the lady has never been uncovered, but if pronounced in East London parlance, Hammersmith becomes Emma Smith, the first Ripper victim. Every time Maybrick heard mention of Hammersmith, the whore Emma returned to haunt him, and inclusion in the Diary would have been a cathartic release within his profoundly disturbed psyche.

'Oh costly intercourse of death', by the poet Richard Crashaw, relating the line *'His Nailes write swords in her'*, in the same poem, leading to the finger nail marks gouged into the stomach of the last Ripper victim, Alice Mackenzie. Here then, within the diary, are obtuse references to both first and last victims, Emma Smith and Alice Mackenzie, a self-gratifying conclusion to the Funny Little Games.

Michael Maybrick, ultimate narcissist, just had to place his achievements on record, cryptically hidden within the script, to exorcise the trauma, congratulate himself on his brilliance, and reassure himself of his invincibility.

So what of the mysterious handwriting? The first twenty four pages of the diary had been cut out, with traces of glue stains on the remaining spine sections indicative of possible use as a scrap book. Was the old diary discovered many years later amongst other household items, and, perhaps in times of economic hardship, used as a scrap book or photo album, on top of the original script? Such occurrences definitely did happen, with one old leger held in a Birkenhead Masonic Lodge testament to the fact, still displaying cut-outs from Victorian times, pasted by children over Masonic entries. The practice was also present in the periods of austerity immediately after both World Wars.

Suppose then, on later discovery of the old leger, and closer inspection of the visible writing, the significance of the contents was realised, and an attempt made to remove the glued items. On assessing the resultant damage, a decision was made to cut out the relevant pages and copy the wording as closely as possible on the remaining pages, with realistic scribbles and scrawls, a task convincingly pursued with evident enthusiasm. Was this a damage limitation exercise to salvage the content of the original, or an opportunity to exploit the financial potential of the diary by passing it off as the untouched genuine article? Perhaps, following the announcement of the discovery, and the ensuing publicity, the contents soon proved too controversial for the person or persons involved to become embroiled in the potentially dangerous and litigious grey area between 'copy' and 'forge'. The controversy continues, but all indications are that an actual record of Jack the Ripper's mindset has been preserved for posterity, word for word, and, ironically, had the diary never been written, the hitherto unassociated Michael Maybrick would never have been exposed as Jack the Ripper. Time really has revealed all.

Maybrick

TEMPUS OMNIA REVELAT.
TIME REVEALS ALL.

Acknowledgements

As a Freemason of over forty years standing, and a longstanding member of James Maybrick's Liverpool Masonic Chapter, my interest in possible connections to the Whitechapel Murders has been ongoing for a similar length of time, inspired by the publication of Shirley Harrison's 'Diary of Jack the Ripper', thereafter pursuing idiosyncrasies and anomalies hitherto unexplored, and deciphering clues left by Michael Maybrick for his own self-gratification. Further inspiration along the way has been provided by Paul Feldman's 'Jack the Ripper, The Final Chapter', and Bruce Robinson's magnificent 'They All Love Jack', both involving in-depth investigation by researcher Keith Skinner. Thanks are due to Robert Smith for words of encouragement over the last couple of years, and gratitude is also extended to the following.

Paul Johnson of the National Archives, Kew. Peter Aitkenhead of the Library and Museum of Freemasonry. The staff at the British Library, Liverpool Central Library, Isle of Wight Council Heritage Service, and the Ryde Social Heritage Group.

Images are published by courtesy of the following:-

∞ Alamy.
∞ Robert Smith.
∞ Look and Learn.
∞ The Museum of Freemasonry.

∞ Tate Images.
∞ The British Library Board.
∞ Isle of Wight Council Heritage Service.
∞ Ryde Social Heritage Group.
∞ The following images are produced by courtesy of the National Archives, Kew. (MEP03-142 pt.1-139) (HO144-1640-A50678/272)

Thanks to Kate Coe of Book Polishers Ltd for invaluable assistance in final co-ordination.

Most importantly, *Funny Little Games* and *The London Medicine* would never have happened without the resilience, perseverance and dedication of my dear wife Elaine, who literally put it all together on the home computer and printer, aided in the final stages by my son Ben. This book is dedicated to you both. Thank you so much.

Book cover design by Ken Dawson of Creative Covers (info@ccovers.co.uk).

Bibliography

Victoria Blake. *Mrs. Maybrick.* National Archives. 2008

Trevor Christie. *Etched in Arsenic.* George Harrop & Co. Ltd. 2005.

Trevor Christie. *The Christie Collection.* University of Wyoming.

Mike Covell. *Jack the Ripper and the Maybrick Family.* Creslivia.. 2015.

Helen Densmore. *The Maybrick Case.* Swan Sonnenschein & Co. 1892.

Richard Deacon. *The Cambridge Apostles.* Farrar, Strauss, Giroux. 1986.

Mervyn Fairclough. *The Ripper and the Royals.* Gerard Duckworthy & Co. Ltd. 1911.

Paul Feldman. *The True History of the Diary of Jack the Ripper.* Virgin Publishing Ltd. 1998.

Anne Graham and Carol Emmas. *The Last Victim.* Headline Book Publishing.1999.

Brian Griffiths and Michael Hedley Hill. *32CCL.* 2005.

Michael Harrison. *Clarence.* W.H. Allen. 1972.

Shirley Harrison. *The Diary of Jack the Ripper.* Smith Gryphon Ltd. 1992.

H.B. Irving. *The Trial of Mrs. Maybrick.* William Hodge & Co. 1912.

J.H. Levy. *The Necessity for Criminal Appeal as Illustrated by the Maybrick Case.* P.K. King & Son. 1899.

Seth Linder, Caroline Morris and Keith Skinner. *Ripper Diary.* The History Press Ltd 2003.

Alexander MacDougall. *The Maybrick Case. A Treatise.* Bailliere, Tyndall & Cox. 1891.

Deborah McDonald. *The Prince, His Tutor and the Ripper.* McFarland & Co. Ltd. 2001.

Florence Elizabeth Maybrick. *My Fifteen Lost Years.* Funk Wagnalls & Co. New York. 1905

Morland Neil. *The Friendless Lady*. Frederick Muller. 1957.

Anthony Plew. *Fidelity, Fidelity, Fidelity*. Author House. 2011.

Bruce Robinson. *They All Have Jack*. Harper Collins. 2015

Robert Smith. *The True History of the Diary of Jack the Ripper*. Mango Books. 2019.

Tobias Smollett. *The Expedition of Humphrey Clinker*. London. 1771.

Chronology

25 October 1838	Birth of James Maybrick
3 January 1841	Birth of Michael Maybrick
4 May 1851	Birth of Edwin Maybrick
3 September 1862	Birth of Florence Maybrick
27 July 1881	Marriage of James and Florence Maybrick
1886	Michael Maybrick joins 20th Middlesex Rifles
4 April 1888	Murder of Emma Smith
7 August 1888	Murder of Martha Tabram
31 August 1888	Murder of Mary Ann Nichols
8 September 1888	Murder of Annie Chapman
30 September 1888	Murder of Liz Stride
30 September 1888	Murder of Catherine Eddowes (Mary Ann Kelly)
9 November 1888	Murder of Mary Jane Kelly
11 May 1889	Death of James Maybrick
14 May 1889	Arrest of Florence Maybrick
17 July 1889	Murder of Alice Mackenzie
7 August 1889	Death sentence on Florence Maybrick
22 August 1889	Reprieve of Florence Maybrick
December 1892	Marriage of Edwin Maybrick
9 March 1893	Marriage of Michael Maybrick
1904	Prison release of Florence Maybrick
26 August 1913	Death of Michael Maybrick
23 October 1941	Death of Florence Maybrick

Index

- Abberline Insp. Frederick — 202, 203, 206, 210, 211, 220
- Addison, John QC — 124, 125, 127, 148, 152, 177
- Albert, Prince Victor — 200, 206, 268
- Alexandra, Princess — 207
- Aunspaugh, Florence — 4, 6, 230
- Barron, Dr Alexander — 55, 146
- Baxendale, Insp. Richard — 56, 57, 60, 67, 68, 77, 80, 81, 89
- Baxter, Coroner Wynne — 106, 110
- Blake, Valentine — 6, 21
- Bond, Dr.Thomas — 111, 112
- Brierley, Alfred — 9, 10, 12, 70, 82, 95, 128
- Brierley, Bessie — 30, 41, 42, 53
- Briggs, Matilda — 9, 35, 53, 58, 59, 101, 177
- Brighouse, Coroner Samuel — 60, 80, 81, 86-89, 93-96, 145
- Brown, Dr. Frederick Gordon — 202
- Bryning, Supt. Isaac — 55, 56, 60, 67, 68, 77, 80, 81, 89, 94, 101, 117, 145

- Cadwallader, Mary — 19, 32, 72
- Callery, Nurse Margaret — 34, 38-44, 152
- Carter, Dr. William — 28, 34-36, 40-43, 52, 55, 74, 82, 94, 99, 132, 133, 146

- Chaucer, Geoffrey — 195
- Crawford, Henry Holmwood — 16
- Cumberland, Stuart — 191-194
- Cleaver, Richard — 61, 62, 67, 77, 95, 124
- Dalglish, John — 61, 62, 86, 89
- Davidson, George — 21, 50, 52, 215-218
- Davies, Edward — 52, 79, 94, 95, 146
- Densmore, Helen — 43, 44, 155, 213, 214
- Dickens, Sir Henry Fielding — 156

- Dones, Arthur 147
- Duckworth, Stella 207
- Euston, Lord 206
- Feldman, Paul 228
- Fleming, Capt. John 3
- Fuller, Dr, Charles 14, 18, 20, 21, 25, 33, 49, 99, 114, 115, 120, 135, 219, 233

- Gorse, Nurse Ellen 24, 38-41, 81, 141, 142
- Graham, Billy 228-232
- Harrison, Shirley 48
- Helen, Princess of Orleans 207
- Hogwood, Mary 1, 3
- Hopper, Arthur 5, 13
- Hughes, Martha 132
- Humphreys, Elizabeth 32, 35, 72
- Humphreys, Dr. Richard 13, 22, 25, 28, 29, 35, 42, 52, 55-61, 76, 94, 129-131, 146

- Iremonger, Sue 48
- Irving, Capt. Peter 28
- Janion sisters 9, 35, 52
- Kelly, Mary Ann 202
- Keuser, Sir Polydore 16
- Knight, John Bailey 10, 11
- Lathom, Earl of 15, 56, 77, 100, 110, 112, 155, 189, 211

- Levy J.H. 42, 99, 185, 186, 190
- Littlechild, Insp. John 211, 220
- Lloyd, Edward 214, 215
- Lowry, Thomas 150
- Lushington, Sir Godfrey 110, 180, 181, 188
- Mackenzie, Alice 101-111
- McDougall, Alexander 44, 45, 53, 72, 118, 133, 134, 141, 142, 147, 179, 190, 191, 211-214

- MacNamara, Dr Rowden — 146
- Mary, Princess of Teck — 208
- Matthews, Sir Henry — 110, 178-182, 189, 223
- May, Lt. Col. H — 225
- Merry, Tom — 178-180
- Morland, Neil — 230
- Muckley, Rembrant. F. — 163-167
- Munro, Comm. James — 112
- Paul, Dr Ralph — 146
- Phillips, Dr. George Bagster — 106-111
- Pickford, William — 77, 81, 86-94, 124, 125, 153
- Quaritch, Bernard Alfred — 199. 200. 224-226
- Ratcliffe, Charles — 169
- Rigg, Morden — 62
- Russell, Sir Charles — 124-142, 148-154, 187
- Sayle, Charles Edward — 199-201
- Schweisso, Alfred — 95, 143, 144, 162
- Sefton, Earl of — 155
- Skinner, Keith — 228, 230
- Smith, Emma — 234
- Smith, George — 19, 20, 50
- Somerset, Lord Arthur — 206
- Stead, William — 196
- Steel, Douglas — 53, 77, 85, 87
- Stephen, James Kenneth — 181, 200, 207, 207
- Stephen, Sir James Fitzjames — 122, 139, 153-162, 168, 200
- Swift, William — 67, 68
- Tennyson, Alfred Lord — 223
- Tidy, Dr. Charles — 146
- Tyrer, Amy — 208, 214
- Von Roques, Baroness Caroline — 60-69, 171-174, 184

- Wales, Prince of 11, 56, 180, 181
- Weatherley, Frederick 209, 226, 227
- Wilson, Nurse 137, 138
- Yapp, Alice 9, 19, 29-35, 51-53, 56, 72-77, 83, 84, 95, 97, 101, 121, 128-141, 162, 165-170, 228-230

N.B.
This list excludes members of the Maybrick family, as this would involve too many references.

www.ingramcontent.com/pod-product-compliance
Lightning Source LLC
Chambersburg PA
CBHW042141160426
43201CB00022B/2368